Daughters of Arraweelo

Stories of Somali Women

AYAAN ADAN

MINNESOTA
HISTORICAL
SOCIETY PRESS

CLEAN WATER LAND & LEGACY AMENDMENT

The publication of this book was supported through a generous grant from the Elmer L. and Eleanor Andersen Publications Fund.

mnhspress.org

The Minnesota Historical Society Press is a member of the Association of University Presses.

Manufactured in the United States of America

10 9 8 7 6 5 4 3 2 1

∞ The paper used in this publication meets the minimum requirements of the American National Standard for Information Sciences— Permanence for Printed Library Materials, ANSI Z39.48–1984.

International Standard Book Number
ISBN: 978-1-68134-182-8 (paperback)
ISBN: 978-1-68134-183-5 (e-book)

Library of Congress Control Number: 2021946296

This and other Minnesota Historical Society Press books are available from popular e-book vendors.

To His Mercy. To His Message. To the Almighty.
To our Creator.

To our light. To our exemplar. To our teacher.
To our Prophet ﷺ.

To my everything.
My family.

Contents

Introduction

Daughters of Arraweelo follows the stories and lives of fourteen Somali women in Minnesota. These women are extraordinary in many ways. We witness their resilience, tenacity, and selflessness as they share their lives and wisdom. They are also ordinary people like you and me. They are moms, students, teachers; they work in health care, tech, law, and politics; they observe the world around them and claim their place in it.

The title of this book refers to Queen Arraweelo, a major figure in Somali mythology. Both her existence and her reputation are debated. Depending on which version you hear, she was either a formidable ruler who antagonized male subjects or a fearsome warrior and defender of the vulnerable. In Somali communities today, girls who are thought to be too assertive are sometimes nicknamed Arraweelo as a disapproving tease. Regardless of how you tell her story, there are themes that remain in various tellings. Arraweelo was headstrong, she cared deeply about her people, and she had strong convictions. The women I spoke to, as varied as they were, shared these traits.

Storytelling allows us to preserve traditions, beliefs, attitudes, proverbs, and feelings. We tell each other who we are, what we fear, and what we aspire to in these stories. I ask you, what are the stories you tell about yourself and the world around you?

I had several goals in taking on this project. First, I wanted to share the stories of dynamic women and hoped many readers could gain from their wisdom. I grew up witnessing resilient men and women use Herculean strength to raise and provide for their families and contribute to their communities. It was commonplace to know someone who performed extraordinary feats to gain better opportunities in life and positively impact innumerable people on their journey. This is how I saw my community. I realized later that my perception was not shared by some outside of my community. It's easy to make boogeymen out of people you don't know. When people try to understand their neighbors by relying on fear-baiting media outlets and politicians with agendas, there are bound to be issues. The unscrupulous can gain a lot of influence and money by dividing people and creating scapegoats. These systems thrive when people are disconnected and consume caricatures about one another.

Newspaper stories, reports, and articles in popular and academic journals often portray innocuous things, such as wearing hijab or performing prayer, as suspicious and worthy of investigation. I knew things were off when I read a story about a young Somali man who was beloved by students, teachers, and parents alike in the school where he worked. In the very last paragraph, the writer wondered why, unlike his peers, the young man was impervious to radicalization. Even in inspiring tales, our stories were inextricably tied to a vile thing. If this sort of reporting is all you consume about a group of people, what might you come to think of them? Equally important, what do these tellings do to the self-image of young Somali Americans, who consistently read and see this coverage about themselves? How do you not internalize what they—strangers—tell you about yourself? What do they tell you is your history? What do they tell you you are? Do you believe them?

Somalis have a rich oral tradition, but we seem to be sharing fewer stories among generations. Families are busy in a globalized, tech-driven world, and storytelling lacks the urgency of overdue bills, long work hours, and constant assessments and assignments. At best, we allow space to grow between us, and at worst, we lose the history traditionally passed on from elders. Those cultural and family stories deserve to keep living. I encourage us to slow down, sit with one another, and enjoy the precious gifts of company and conversation. I hope future generations use these stories as a window into the migration, identities, and lives of the Somali diaspora.

Through the process of collecting these stories, I also hoped to better understand myself. By listening, exploring, and examining the stories of these women, I sought to find my own voice. I came to learn that I shared joy, pain, anger, humor, fears, and love with the women I interviewed. In each interview, I learned a little more about myself and about the world around me. I gained stronger empathy for my mother and for other women and girls in my life.

∼

I interviewed Somali women of three generations: young women who were born in the United States or primarily raised here, women who arrived in the States as teenagers and juggled two worlds, and elders who can tell stories about colonialism, democracy and revolution, war and displacement. I turned those interviews into first-person stories. I worked closely with the women to get those stories right.

Some of the women chose to contribute publicly, while others chose to use pseudonyms. In pseudonymous stories, any names, places, or relationships mentioned have most likely been changed.

In the tradition of nonfiction writers, I was given an extraordinary responsibility. The subjects are real. The stories are real. How do I do justice to these women and their stories? How do I balance presenting the extraordinary aspects of their lives without sensationalizing their stories? How do I deal with sensitive topics? How do I bring their texture and dimensionality to life in words? I admit I still don't have the answers, but I learned the tremendous importance of having the guts to follow the story and the humility to acknowledge what I do not know. The process called for measured respect, collaboration, and the wisdom to realize that this project was both calling to me and bigger than me.

I struggled to not let my own biases and interpretations dilute or manipulate the pure stories of my subjects. I have tried to be as objective as possible in both interviews and storytelling.

⁓

I went into these conversations expecting to interrogate the vast array of opinions held by the different generations and to get to the sources of misunderstanding among them. I know: an arrogant and presumptuous goal. And what I found genuinely took me by surprise. The contributors differed not only from generation to generation but from woman to woman. No two people were alike. Of course! I naively thought each person would stick to their respective team and share a general opinion held by their peers. Instead, there was no universal view or unanimous perspective. The women, in all their sophistication, were complicated, both passionate and coherent in their conclusions. They contrasted with each other and spoke with great clarity and assurance about their beliefs and stories. I was captivated.

Everyone held their own. The youth are filled with emotion, conviction, and uncertainty, and they're trying to make sense of the world around them using the tools they have. Those in the middle generation, having experienced both worlds, are cultural bridges and act as guides for other generations to understand one another and appreciate differences. They have empathy for other generations, and they're trying to find their way. And the elders hold a lifetime of wisdom, delivered bluntly and without cushion but with discernment and goodwill. Knowledge and life lessons are shared by each person. Everyone adds value. I was interested as both a writer and a person. What would they say next? What do they think of this? How do they see that? They brought their whole selves, backed by a lifetime of experience, insight, and fascinating stories.

These women were more alike than different. They are worlds apart in upbringing, identity, and experience, and yet they relate to each other more than they might have assumed. They are fiercely passionate about their faith, family, and friends. They often reflect on their greater purpose and the legacy they would leave behind. They share their vulnerabilities and fears, and they immediately remember what brought them gratitude and joy.

Does that sound familiar? It should, because these are all of our stories. These are the universal and timeless themes of human nature.

We create understanding when we are able to share stories and learn from one another. Each of our paths in life is unique, and yet the human experience is universal. We all know and can find ourselves in curiosity, striving, devotion, hurt, anger, fear, generosity, and love. My intention is to share the positivity of and a love for the craft of storytelling. In the words of the great Fyodor Dostoevsky, "But how could you live and have no story to tell?"

If nothing else, I hope you find a good story in the pages that follow. And for a little while, you lose yourself in the magic of a book.

1

Aisha Musse, 20s, Mombasa, Kenya
pseudonym

I was born in Mombasa, Kenya. I am the firstborn of my parents. My mom was most worried about my birth. As I was her first pregnancy and birth, she was scared of what could happen to her. My dad got a call from the hospital of my mom's labor and was so excited, he began running to the hospital instead of driving the car he had. He missed my birth but was there soon after. My mom was very close to her midwife, an Arab woman named Aisha—so much so that I was named after her. Aisha is also the name of a wife of the Prophet Muhammad ﷺ and is an Arabic name meaning *living* or *prosperous*. My mom has a habit of wanting to make the people around her happy; I think that's in part why I was named after her midwife. It's a trait we both share.

I grew up hearing so many stories about my grandfather. He died the year I was born. I can't imagine what that was like for my mom. In spring, she welcomed life, and by fall, she mourned the greatest man she ever knew. My grandfather was a noble man. He was in the military, a general who commanded respect. He had a dream of building a legacy for his descendants to come. He built a grand estate for his large family in our hometown of Kismaayo. He had five or six wives and many children. My maternal grandmother would say that women were his weakness. My mom had eight full siblings and many more half-siblings. She was my grandfather's only daughter and his favorite. Awoowe lived a full life. He lived through Italian colonization, Somalia's independence, and short-lived democracy. A nation coming into its own. Later in his life, and before the war, the Siad Barre administration asked him to become an advisor. After much thought, my grandfather declined the offer. He wanted his remaining years to be simple and religious.

He was ahead of his time in many ways. He demanded that his daughter and other girls become educated. He insisted that his daughter's sex would not become her handicap and that she was just as smart as his sons. He also made sure his sons engaged in domestic work and was mocked for it by anyone who would visit and see boys preparing meals or washing clothes. He was viewed as eccentric at the time, but it didn't matter to him. He was a man of conviction, and once he believed in something, there was no convincing him otherwise.

He, like most of my family, eventually had to flee the war. He was a very old man by then, and he never imagined dying anywhere but Somalia, but they had no choice but to flee to Kenya. He died the year I was born. His body was sent back to be buried in his estate. My grandmother went home many years later and found the estate completely destroyed. Most of it lay in rubble. Neighbors told her stories of how the compound was used as a place for soldiers to rape women and hide out. Bloodstains were still visible on the stone; bullet holes marred what remained. It pained me to hear my grandfather's legacy, his life's work, had been reduced to something so brutal. Had been reduced to rubble. Had been abused as he lay in rest. If I could have anything in the world, I would go home and rebuild my grandfather's estate. If not as a home for our family, then as a boarding school for girls and boys, to continue his legacy.

Because my mom was my grandfather's only daughter, he was very protective of her. He had high hopes for his daughter. She was only a teenager when the war broke out. Her safe home had turned into a nightmare. Gunshots rang throughout the night. My elderly grandfather was the only man left at the estate to protect his wives and children. Anything could happen at nighttime when the most action broke out. The women were afraid of being raped by soldiers and the men of being shot dead. Awoowe had to hire neighborhood boys to watch over the estate at night to keep the family safe. One day my mom and cousin saw a bus approaching filled with people and all their worldly possessions. My mom looked at my cousin and looked back at the bus. She made a split-second decision to get on the bus and flee. She told her cousin to tell her parents that she was alive, because their first instinct when she didn't come home that night would be to believe that she had been killed.

My mom had no idea where the bus was taking her. She only knew that she had to live, and in order to live, she had to get out while she could. The bus drove through old neighborhoods in the city. Neighborhoods she had known like the lines of her palms. She witnessed bodies piled on top of bodies. Blood everywhere, the stench emanating through the air. She started to recognize the corpses in the streets. Her old macalin, a childhood friend, a neighbor—the list went on and on. She began to numb herself to the horror around her. Once she got off that bus, she was never the same. It still haunts her, but she keeps the memories to herself. A burden only she can bear.

The bus took her to a refugee camp in Kenya. That's where she met my dad. My dad is a Sujuu Somali, native to Kenya. Sujuu Somalis are Somalis who have lived in Kenya for generations. They have their own dialect and unique traditions. My dad taught himself English. He was a polyglot and worked as an interpreter for the UN. He spoke English, Somali, and Swahili. He met my mom when he was interpreting for her. Let my dad tell it: it was love at first sight. He was captivated by her beauty. Pretty soon, they fell in love and he proposed. My mom's family didn't want her to marry him. My awoowe was a respected man from a powerful tribe and had big hopes for his only daughter. Many wealthy and influential men had asked for her hand. She could have anyone she wanted. And instead, she chose this unknown Sujuu interpreter from Kenya. My mom had to fight for their marriage, and in the end she got what she wanted.

In hindsight, my mom was dealing with war and displacement and was in an unstable chapter in her life. She rushed into marriage in the chaos of it all. She also wanted an opportunity to leave Kenya. My dad could offer her life in America, where they could build something for themselves. So she took the chance. My mom always says, "Dhanta aa igu qastay." Necessity or fate forced me. When they lived together in Kenya, they would constantly house guests passing through or seeking asylum. It was in their nature as Somalis. The war brought out the worst of some people, but it brought out the best in others. People went out of their way to be kind to one another and look out for other Somalis who could be complete strangers to them. That's the Somali way.

My parents divorced when I was three years old. My parents never told me the story; I overheard from chatty aunties growing up. Mom went to America first with just me and eventually ended up in Minnesota. The plan was for my dad to work for a couple years for the UN and Mom would later sponsor him. Dad sent money from his good UN job. Eventually, the money my dad sent became less and less. My mom was suspicious, but she chalked it up to his relatives needing more money. Soon after, my dad began asking my mom indirectly if he could bring someone with him. My mom would question who he would want to bring, but he would never say who. My mom started to get more worried over time. She started working in the States, earning an income while raising me. She was a hustler, got that from her dad. One day, her aunt called from Kenya, saying she saw Dad with a young Arab woman. The gossip back home had finally arrived at Mom's doorstep. My mom applied pressure on my dad and found out that Dad had gotten a second wife behind her back. My mom was mortified. This is the man she went to war for. This is the man she disobeyed her father for. The man whose child she was raising by herself in a foreign country. And this is what he does to her? Worse yet: he lied to her. Dishonesty was one thing my mother could never tolerate. She absolutely couldn't stand for it. They divorced shortly after. My mother would say, "Dhanta aa igu qastay."

I am the oldest of eleven siblings. I am the only child born of my father and mother. For that reason, I've always felt a loneliness with my siblings. None of them could fully relate to me. And I had no one to confide in about my unique problems. My mom remarried eventually, and my father came to America with his new wife. I lived with my mom exclusively and rarely saw my dad. I was relegated to the role of third parent for my siblings. I helped raise them, discipline them, and comfort them. This warped my relationship with my siblings. They didn't see me as one of them. Especially when my mom would compare them to me, the model student and child. My sister Fadumo went through a rebellious phase and her grades suffered for it. She grew to resent me when Mom would yell at her to get it together: "Why can't you be like Aisha?" This was a wedge in our relationship. When I got older, I told my mom to stop comparing me to them. It was not good for them, and it didn't have the intended effect. When I got older, my mom and stepdad would both come to me for advice on how to deal with the rest of the kids. I had an advisor role. Stuck in the middle, knowing what my parents wanted and understanding what my siblings were experiencing. I was teaching them how to be better parents to my siblings. The irony wasn't lost on me.

∽

My K–12 experience could be summarized in one word: violent. I was an avid reader and an excellent student, but I got into a lot of fights no matter where I went. I was bullied for whatever was the flavor of the week. For standing out, being chubby, being a Muslim, wearing hijab, being Somali, African, Black—you decide! When I went to school with lots of Somalis, I was bullied for being chubby and was called an Oreo. I never initiated a single fight but always stood up for myself. I couldn't let anyone talk down to me, so I would fight back. The bullying was getting so bad that my mom noticed and worried about me. She was getting called down to my school so often that I couldn't even hide the fights if I wanted to. My mom pulled me out of that school eventually.

I went to a predominantly White middle school with some Asian and Black students and was bullied consistently. I was not a fighter, but I had to learn to be. If I didn't fight back, I would get my ass beat at home by my mom. I would get my hijab yanked off in the hallways. I had to constantly be vigilant. On the bus, no one wanted to sit next to Somalis. We were nicknamed "Smellyians," and it became a taboo to even share a seat with us. The bus ride was a place of anxiety. For a while, my cousins rode the bus with me, so we could always count on each other to defend ourselves. Eventually they moved to another school district and I was by myself, the only Somali kid on the bus. One day, the bus was at near full capacity. There were two spots left. One with a Cambodian girl and the other an African American girl. The Cambodian girl had her backpack and foot on the seat to prevent me from sitting there. I tried to sit down, and she pushed me off the seat. Then I tried to sit with the Black girl, and she also pushed me off. At this point, I was desperate. This was the last seat on the bus. I had to fight for it. I tried to sit with her again, and she pushed me off. We entered a silent pushing war; neither one of us said a word as we shoved each other. She won and managed to push me off a third time.

Picture me, a lone ten-year-old Somali girl in the middle of winter at 6:00 in the morning fighting for a seat on a bus. I was exhausted and didn't want to keep fighting. I resigned myself to sitting on the slush-soaked, muddy bus floor. The White bus driver looked me dead in the eye as I sat on the floor and looked away, refusing to intervene for the duration of the twenty-five-minute bus ride. The other kids noticed me on the floor and begin pointing and name-calling. They snickered, "Look at the Smellyian sitting on the floor!" The entire bus erupted in laughter. The Cambodian girl who had refused me a seat laughed the hardest of all. It was then that it really hit me that I didn't belong anywhere. Not with the Somalis, Asians, Blacks, or Whites. Not with anyone. I could never tell my mom about the bus incident. For one, she would beat my ass for not fighting those girls. And then she would go to my school and raise hell. It was already bad enough to be humiliated by the entire bus; no way was I gonna add in another ass whooping and be embarrassed on campus. I hid a lot of fights from my mom. But I had to learn which fights to pick. At our school, if Black kids fought each other, our teacher would resolve it. But let me stand up to a White or Asian bully, and I would be sent to the principal and get suspended. Black students knew who was protected and who could get touched.

The high school I attended was a mostly Hmong school. There was a major difference in how Hmong students versus Black students were treated. It was the unspoken rule. We were punished more harshly and always met with suspicion and apprehension by the school staff, especially the SROs. Student resource officers are cops who are placed in the school by the district through its contracts with the police department. The assumption is that cops make schools safer. This could not be further from the truth. SROs are, at their core, cops. They are trained to escalate situations using violence. They carry weapons and are quick to use them on Black students.

I saw this firsthand in my school. One day I was having lunch with my friends, Michael and Ty. They got into an argument and stood up as they got more and more upset. They had not even placed hands on each other before two SROs came charging down the cafeteria. The SROs pushed them both. One SRO jumped on my friend Michael and threw him to the ground. The SRO held him down and placed a knee on his neck. A crowd of students had formed, and we were shouting for the SRO to get off Michael, but he wouldn't listen. The crowd became scared and silent as Michael shouted that he couldn't breathe and that he was gonna die. The SRO laughed it off and told him to shut up. "Who told you to fight? Shut up! Who told you to be disruptive?" said the SRO. Michael already had asthma, and he turned purple as he was losing air. At that moment, he wasn't a sixteen-year-old kid; he was a Black man. He was a threat.

It wasn't until our older White principal came out and told the SRO to get off Michael or he was fired that he finally took his knee off of Michael. Someone found Michael's inhaler in his book bag as he gasped for air. Eventually an ambulance was called to take Michael away to get medical care. He was never the same again. We all thought he was gonna die. That SRO was eventually fired, but their abuse launched a student-led campaign to end SROs in school.

It was my first foray into activism. We met with teachers, the school board, and anyone who would listen. We fought hard and were denied at every turn. It wasn't until the murder of George Floyd that St. Paul Public Schools ended their contract with the police department. I cried when I found out. I felt relieved that students would no longer be terrorized by cops in their school. But I was also angry. Why had it taken so long? My friend Michael could have been killed the exact same way George Floyd was killed. Did his life not matter? I carry that anger for him. A sixteen-year-old boy who lost his innocence of the world and nearly his life all at once.

When I graduated high school, I was determined to go to an HBCU. I was so happy when I was accepted into Howard University, my dream school. Unfortunately, the out-of-state tuition and cost was too strong a barrier. I enrolled in a local college that I could afford. My mom wanted me to be a doctor, and I wanted to make her happy. I chose the premed major and hated it immediately. I switched to nursing and also hated that. Medicine was not for me. This is when I had to stand up to my mom and start to make my own way. I remembered a sociology course I loved in high school and switched majors for a final time.

I joined student groups and local activist organizations. I learned about grassroots organizing and how to create change through movements powered by people. I learned firsthand about the sexism women face in leadership positions. How our leadership is constantly questioned. I learned that, more than anything else, women have to worry about being liked and about how we come off. And as a Muslim woman leader, my views, politics, and goals are assumed to be suspect, and I am presumed to be an unqualified radical by virtue of being a woman. There's a lot that we're up against, just to make effective change in our community and the world around us. We have to work that much harder to cancel the noise, just to be heard and to do the things we came to do.

By the time I graduated from college, I had a firm direction for my career. I wanted to help people: that was a definite requisite of my mom that I followed without resistance. And I care about education and young people. I'm now in a program where I help connect students to resources. I know I want to go back to school for my doctorate. I want to make change for students on a grand scale. That's why I want to help young people. I'm tired of appealing to people who don't care about us and can't relate to our experiences. Students deserve better.

◜◞

My mom was very serious about prayer when we were growing up. If we didn't pray fajr, we wouldn't get breakfast. This harsh approach to prayer did not have its intended effect. It actually gave me a skewed perception of our Creator as angry and unforgiving. There was such a focus on punishment and fear that it wasn't until I was older that I learned about Illahi's mercy and love. Even though my mom was very strict on prayer, she had a lackadaisical attitude toward hijab. For the most part, we wore what we wanted to wear. I started wearing hijab in third grade because I wanted to look like the women around me. It wasn't until I was older that I developed a true appreciation for its purpose.

I think my mom's attitude toward hijab was due to her own upbringing. My grandparents were strict on my mom about wearing hijab at a young age. My mom never wanted to repeat that ordeal with us, but in the process she switched one thing for another. That's the thing about parents. They can only parent the way they know. In the masjids, I remember watching grown women in niqabs openly backbite in the musallah. It would be easy to understand if I held on to that skewed perception of my faith because of the imperfect, hypocritical Muslims I witnessed. But I'm grateful that Allah (سبحانه وتعالى) gave me the gift of discernment that allowed me to understand the difference between the religion He sent and the imperfect people who received the message. I never judged Islam by the behavior of Muslims.

As a Muslim in the States, I am prouder of my faith because it's something I fought for. It's not easy being a Muslim here because we go against the grain. Our beliefs, traditions, and customs are not always popular, and in fact, depending on who you talk to, Islam is very disliked and hated. It reminds me of a hadith where the Prophet Muhammad ﷺ was to have said, "A time of patience will come to people in which adhering to one's religion is like grasping a hot coal" (Sunan al-Tirmidhī, 2260). It feels like that's never been more true than now. In this time and place, we have so much fitnah we're facing: Islamophobes, surveillance, social media, and more. We are overwhelmed. To continue to openly and unapologetically practice our faith is brave, especially as Muslim women who wear hijabs. When it's my time to pass, I want to be buried in Medina so I can be resurrected with the Prophet ﷺ and his companions. If not there, I want to be buried next to my grandfather so I may be resurrected with him.

I am a Black Muslim woman, a Somali American. My Somali identity is the one I'm most connected to. The thing about Somali people is that we get so much hate. Every time Trump came to Minnesota to stir up support, he was sure to remind people of how much they should hate Somalis. Why? We are such a small number of people; how do we hold this much power in the mind of the president? Or the people who claim we're ruining America? I think Somalis get so much hate because we will never fully assimilate. Our names are uncomfortable in Americans' mouths, our clothes are bright and patterned, visibly different from the sea of blue jeans and T-shirts. We're different. But not only are we different: we are proud to be ourselves. How dare we? Every time a racist or Islamophobe looks at Somalis, they are reminded of our refusal to be broken. We created our own subculture in America. I'm proud of my people. I hope we don't cave to the pressure of conforming and lose all that we created.

~

My mom is the most complicated person in the history of my life. I am in awe of her strength and resilience in all that she's done for me and my siblings. She's managed to make a home in a country far away from home. My mom tried harder with me than with any other child. When I was trying to figure out a way to finance my education, my mom stepped up and said "we" will find a way to pay for it. I don't want to accept it. I know how hard my mom works, and I feel guilty enough not contributing. Past a certain age as an eldest child, we know that we should be helping our parents and easing their burden, not adding to it. But my mom told me that she and I have no one in this world but each other. Because my father is not around, she works extra hard for me to not notice his absence. She said my siblings have both their parents in their lives; they'll be fine. But she will be there for me in every capacity and for as long as I need it. She always made sure I had nice clothes and the latest gadgets, in a way that I knew was not the reality for my friends I grew up with. She overcompensated on those material things as she tried to make up for what I didn't have in a father.

And yet I feel like I've always grappled with two versions of my mother. One who loved me and protected me, and one who hurt me. When I would disagree with her or act out, she would threaten to take me to my father's house. My mom would throw in my face that my own father didn't want me. So where would I go? Because of that, I had this instability growing up, a home built on a shaky foundation. My safety and home depended on how I behaved or my mother's mood that day. Only one of those I could control; the rest was not up to me. My mom did to me what she was trying to protect me from. She magnified the absence of my father in my life to an undeniable degree.

It scarred me in ways I am still working on healing from. I discovered the power of journaling and used it as a tool to uncover my memories and examine my emotions. Not long after, I started seeing a therapist to manage my mental health. My mom was not shy about her disapproval. She felt that admitting I needed help from a therapist was the same thing as admitting that I'm weak. She tells me to just pray if I'm feeling a type of way. She sees my problems as an exaggeration of reality. *Were things really that bad? Was I such a bad mom?*

But as I've grown older, I've learned that my healing and mental health have to come first. Stigma and misconceptions be damned. Therapy has helped me to identify unhealthy behaviors and patterns and to have a safe space to confront, accept, and heal from my traumas and fears. It's helped me grow as a person. And because I have no one in my family and friends circle who can relate to my life as an only child of my parents and the unique circumstances of my upbringing, it's nice to have a place to speak safely and be free from judgment and alienation. Healing is not a linear path, but it's one that must have a starting point somewhere. I've started my journey, and I can't wait to see the woman that I will become.

~

I can count on my hands the number of times I saw my dad as I was growing up. He lived only a couple hours away. He started a new family with his second wife. My mom used to call me "agoon" when I was a kid, and I hated it. But she was right. He would call me whenever he moved. But the calls became fewer and further between, until he had gone ten years without calling or seeing me. My dad was out of my life for so long that I would tell the kids at school that my dad died of cancer. Somehow that was easier to explain than our reality. And deep down, I started to believe he was dead. That was easier to accept than his willful absence.

My mom never collected child support from my dad. She asked him for something only one time. She asked him once before he disappeared if he would come and get me my passport, because the state required his permission as my parent. By then, I hadn't seen him in years. We went to get my passport, and afterward he took me to McDonald's. He bought me four chicken nuggets and a water. In front of him sat his firstborn, the one whose birthdays, recitals, parent-teacher conferences, baby teeth, and first steps he missed, and this is all the effort he put in. He couldn't even try to buy my love. In fact, he's never bought me a single gift. I came to find that my father was stingy. He was stingy with his money, his time, and, most of all, his love.

I called him one day before his disappearance and found his line had been disconnected. No one knew where he went. My mom didn't talk about him. I would eavesdrop on my nosy aunts, but even they were at a loss. I became obsessed. There were periods of time when I would look him up every day in the white pages. I searched the web. I looked through newspapers. I searched fervently. I feared that perhaps my father had died and no one had told me. Fate could not be so cruel, could it? To be called an orphan and then to be made one.

A few years ago, I decided to make dua that I may find my father. It was during the holy month of Ramadan. All of my prayers had been accepted and come true the past Ramadan. I would make dua before fajr, before I broke my fast, and during tarawix. I prayed, "Oh Allah, please make it easy for me to find him. Please make him remember me, the child he forgot."

During the last ten nights of Ramadan, one of my mom's distant cousins in Kismaayo got a call from a relative in California. He told her that he saw a man who resembled the picture of her niece that she had sent him, Aisha. He saw this man at a masjid and wanted to know if he should approach him. She told him to get his number, and then he called my mom and gave us my dad's phone number. I cried when I found out my prayer had been answered.

Allah (سبحانه وتعالى) went through people I didn't even know to answer my dua. He went across continents. Someone might see the extraordinary amount of chance behind this miracle and think it was by luck. But I know it was fate. And it was because of my duas. Allah (سبحانه وتعالى) is capable of anything and is not limited by our imagination. I am still in awe of His power and what He could do for me.

I reconnected with my dad. I wanted to know him because I wanted to know the other half of myself. My dad's absence left me with a lot of questions and a lot of pain. I wanted a chance to heal those scars and move on. I also wanted to know my siblings before we became old and completely distant. They were young and didn't know me. The following year, I decided to visit my dad and meet my siblings and stepmom. I fantasized about meeting my dad for years. I thought it would be like a movie. I was full of butterflies. When my mom found out I was visiting my dad, she didn't speak to me for three months. For her, it was a slap in the face. She did everything she could for me growing up, and I repaid her by visiting this man who did not so much as take me to a playground once. I understood her anger and hurt, but he was still my dad, and I had a right to know him.

Making this extraordinary effort to locate and have a relationship with my dad required a lot of healing on my own. My parents were young refugees when they got married. I made every excuse in my head for my deadbeat dad. He was young, he didn't know how to love, he had PTSD, he was broken, he was damaged, he was old-fashioned, he didn't know how to be a father.

Nothing hurt me more than finding out that he was a good father—just not to me. My siblings called him "baba" and would wait by the door for him to come home. He cooked dinner for them, asked them how they were, played with them, cleaned their house, and provided for them. He was a girl-dad. He would plop his daughters in front of him and tenderly braid their hair. He was a super-dad. He was physically and emotionally present for his kids. He was better than I could have ever imagined. How could he love them so much and not show me one percent of that? One day of love? One hour of love? My stepmom showed me family photo albums. Family vacations they had gone on together, memories they made, school pictures. The amazing life my dad had built for my siblings.

I was in disbelief. My system was shocked. I immediately internalized it. How could his absence not be about me, if I am the only child he forgot? The only child he never loved, the only child he left behind? My heart was broken. I think my dad wanted to talk to me because he knew I had seen how he was with them and how he's been with me. He wanted to get ahead of it and get everything out in the open.

My dad took me out to dinner and tried to get me to open up and talk to him. It was too late. I became numb to the pain and shut down. I stayed in my room and skipped meals. I called my mom and tried to get a return flight ASAP. I couldn't last this trip. The reality I created in my mind to excuse my dad and protect myself came burning down. My stepmom came into my room one day and tried to have a heart-to-heart. She wanted me to know that my dad was in pain and wanted me to forgive him. I couldn't believe what I was hearing. Who was she to tell me to forgive my father? I could never relate to her. It was never her responsibility to make my dad be a father, but how could she be with a man and have kids by him knowing how unkind he was to his own child? I would never let my husband forget his obligations to his children. She didn't owe me anything, but she sure as hell did not have the right to emotionally manipulate me into forgiving my dad and trying to have a relationship with him. She had twenty-some years to convince *him* to have a relationship with me.

My dad took me out to dinner again. It was a holiday; restaurants were closed. We ended up at a Sonic and parked somewhere with our food. It was awkward between us. This man was a stranger to me. Everything that a relationship with a father shouldn't be. This time, he didn't try to get me to open up. Instead, he had written me a letter. He read it to me. He told me he remembered the day I was born and the excitement he had for my birth. He became emotional when he talked about holding me in his arms the first time and the feeling of fierce love that overcame him. He said he never intended to leave my mother and for the situation to be how it was. He regretted walking away from me when he walked away from my mother. He told me about his horrible childhood and how his stepmom was abusive and vicious toward him. She hid her cruelty toward her stepchildren, and my dad shared traumatic story after traumatic story detailing his abuse. He vowed to never let his children endure the cruelty of a stepparent, and even though he loved his wife, he could never allow me to endure the same fate. He wanted me to be raised by my mom because only she could protect and love me the way a mother could. "I wanted to be in your life and protect you, but I failed as a man." He apologized with tears in his eyes. I was speechless. He gave me permission to yell at him, to hit him, to do anything at all, because he was frightened by my silence. I had been so quiet during my stay that he was worried about my well-being. I remained silent as he shared his story.

I couldn't believe his words. The numbness that restrained me was starting to be eclipsed by raw anger and disbelief. This was his excuse? This was the elaborate excuse that he had twenty-some years to concoct? And he was worried about me? He cared now? Not during the ten years he didn't speak to me or see me. Not during the graduations he missed. Not during the anguish and turmoil he had caused. Not when it mattered. But now? I felt like I was in a movie again. Except this time, this was the dramatic scene where the undeserving, deadbeat dad admits his guilt and begs for forgiveness from his perfect and successful kid. Only this wasn't a movie. This was real life, my life. My dad's letter slowly tipped over the bottle of emotion I had kept deep inside of me and away from sunlight or peering eyes.

I turned to my dad and said, "I have nothing to say to you. I dreamt about this day. I thought about it almost every single day of my life. I thought about what I would say to you. I thought about what our reunion would be like. You are capable of being a good father, but you chose to not be a good father to me. I don't care what anyone did to you. You had the chance to make sure that that trauma and pain ended with you, but you chose to pass it on to me. To abandon me and hurt me. That was your choice. It would be easier for me to forgive you if you were not capable of being a loving father who can fulfill his responsibilities, but clearly you are. You go above and beyond for your other children, when you couldn't fulfill even one obligation toward me. You're the reason I'm in pain. You're the reason I'm scared of marriage. You're the reason I can't trust men.

"I hate you. I have no desire to ever talk to you again. After this trip, you will never hear from me again, don't worry. You don't have to put up with that anymore. I came looking for answers, and I found everything I needed to know. Allahu Akbar. I hope you have a good rest of your life. Know that when you die, I am not coming to your funeral. If I die before you, don't come to mine."

My dad began sobbing hysterically. I never saw a grown Somali man cry like that before, showing emotion in this vulnerable way. He told me it was okay and that he understood. And he continued to cry. When I saw him sobbing like a child, my humanity and naxaariis for my father returned to me. I consoled him. The roles had reversed. Like so much of my childhood, I played his part and he mine. Him, absentminded in a way only a child could be, unwilling to see the consequences of his actions. Me, chasing a man who should never have needed to be chased and trying to have a relationship with a man who destroyed our home and replaced me with others. I told him it was okay, even though it wasn't. I told him it wouldn't be roses and butterflies, but to give it time, and that if he was serious, he had a lot to make up for. He had missed a lot of years, and he had a lot to answer for.

I say Alhamdulilah for that conversation with my father. I know that a lot of immigrant girls will never be able to have such a conversation with their dads who hurt them. If they spoke the way I spoke to my dad, they would be yelled at for being disrespectful. We're not allowed to talk to our parents like that; it's a respect thing. But speaking honestly allowed me to have the closure I was looking for. Yes, my dad was a deadbeat, but at least he recognized his own failing and didn't try to gaslight me. It's still a process. This journey has not been linear. I still harbor a lot of negative emotions toward him, but I'm working through it by the power of Allah (سبحانه وتعالى). I'm in the process of healing from an intergenerational trauma. Because if I have any power over it, it will stop with me.

When I visit my dad now, he tries to hang out with me and spend time together. It's awkward. It feels unnatural and uneasy. There aren't memories or inside jokes to revisit, no shared nostalgia for days past. He doesn't know me, and I don't really know him. The discomfort is palpable, thick enough to cut. There's also a part of me that is mad that he wants to spend time together now, and not when I needed him. That we are on his time. It's more for him than for me at this point. So why force it? Yet I try. I'm not entirely sure why. I'm still working this out with God. I'm grateful that throughout all this Allah (سبحانه وتعالى) has proven to be most constant and unwavering. I've leaned on Him more times than I can count. So perhaps a part of me is doing this for His sake.

∼

To my Somali people, first of all, thank you. It is because of you that I am who I am today. You have created a strong, resilient woman who knows and loves her diin and culture. I don't know who I'd be if I was in any other culture. I love us. I love everything about us and everything we stand for. I'm incredibly grateful to dadka Soomaaliyeed, through their faults and all, for helping me become the person I am today.

To the Somali women who came before us, I see you and I know that you're trying your best. I forgive you for your shortcomings, and I hope you will forgive yourself too. You're a human being who is capable of making mistakes. I'm sorry you've had to be so strong. I will never fully know what you've experienced to bring us here. I want you to know that your struggle was not in vain. We young women will learn from you and be better for it. We will heal ourselves, be intentional about our story, pick better spouses and fathers for our children, take our time, and raise a generation that is kinder, wiser, and better people than we were. This will happen because of you. No matter what age you are, it is never too late to heal. Find healing through whatever works for you, be it poetry, conversation, Qur'an, or whatever you find.

To Somali girls, don't ever settle. The person you allow into your life to love you and be loved by you will be the father of your children. This is bigger than you; it's an amanah. Love alone is not enough. Respect, compatibility, stability, diin, and others are factors. If love is the only basis, you set yourself up for failure. Our mothers went through what they went through as physical lessons in what not to put up with. Our moms may not have had a choice, out of necessity. But we're educated and have the opportunity to learn from their mistakes.

To Somali boys and men, I love you. I hold you to a high standard because I know you can reach it. This comes from a place of love and caring about you. I will never talk down on our men to ajnabi people. Our men are a reflection of us and we of them. I want you to know that I know you're capable of doing better and being better.

To the man who didn't raise me, I forgive you so I can forgive me. I am not going to be stuck in this perpetual cycle of trauma with you. I choose peace. I choose me.

To the man I will one day marry, get ready for me. I'm a lot, but I'm worth it.

To the men I will one day raise, I love you. You have a tough mom who loves you. You are allowed to cry. You are allowed to speak about love and to be loved. You will be strong, because strength is not the absence of emotion.

2

Habon Hirsi, 20s, Seattle, Washington

pseudonym

I was born in Seattle, but we moved to Minneapolis when I was small. I am the first and only child of both of my parents. They split when I was just a baby, and then they both went on to remarry and have more kids. I grew up with five siblings, and I have another seven siblings from my dad's side that I wasn't raised with. The community in Seattle was small and more tight-knit than others. Because of that, Somali people looked to one another for support and had a familiarity and camaraderie. My mom was originally going to name me Hibaq, which means guidance. But not long before I was born, the storyteller in our neighborhood persuaded her to name me Habon instead. The man was an elder, a respected one whose name we couldn't tell you. The closeness of our community lent itself to that level of trust and respect. I was named by a stranger.

My parents are from the same town on the southern coast of Somalia. They knew of each other's families back home but didn't know each other personally. They came to the States young, naive, and full of hope. My mom came alone without any family or knowing relatives in this new country. I am blown away by her resilience and determination. My dad worked odd jobs and drove a taxi. Mom worked in retail.

In order to understand my mother better, you have to understand her past. My maternal grandparents split up, and that left my mom in an unstable position. She had no one to take care of her and had to make it on her own. She ultimately raised herself. She struggled to survive, traveling to Kenya to find work. She was a maid and was mistreated by the family that employed her.

She had to do a lot on her own. I wish we had conversations about her upbringing earlier. It sheds light on the nature of some of our disagreements through the years. Perhaps she didn't have many examples to draw on because she had no one but herself for a tumultuous period. My mom is protective and stubborn, traits that seem inevitable given the life she lived. I don't think often about what would have happened if we didn't go through the Civil War. But from time to time, my mind lingers on my mother's upbringing and family. I imagine how it has affected us in ways we don't yet fully grasp. Had the Civil War not erupted, perhaps our people would have been closer. But maybe the war showed how divided we were underneath. Maybe it's not the cause but a symptom of our condition.

My siblings mean the world to me. The pandemic brought us closer together and showed us how petty our ritual grievances and arguments were. We all had to lean on each other to get through mentally. Home is where I feel comfortable, where I can be myself. My brothers and sisters are my home. When I am with them, I can completely be myself; I feel at peace, safe, and loved. Home is many things, but I could not place a geographical location. Even though I've only ever known Minneapolis for most of my life, this isn't home; it's my circumstance. Home is not solely where you grew up; it's also where you decide to stay. For many years, I dreamt of living elsewhere. Then I could give myself some time to feel homesick, to long for a place where I know the city and the people who make it home.

∾

Tribalism is a contentious topic in our community. It has divided people for more years than I could guess. At the school I attended, most kids were Ogaden. At the masjid I attended, most kids were Majeerteen. Minnesota is a state that is predominantly Darood. The tribe I belong to does not have a major presence in Minnesota. Regardless, tribe is not something that my mom prioritized in our household. In fact, I didn't even know what tribe I belonged to until an incident at dugsi.

My friends and I were gathered, chatting about trivial things in hushed tones, trying to avoid the ire of macalamiin and quick-tempered moms. We were as thick as thieves, but one day a friend said, "Whoever is X-tribe, I'm gonna beat their ass. They could never be around me." I didn't know the name of my tribe, but I knew it started with the same letter she said. I looked at her and asked with hesitation, "What if I'm that tribe?" She paused before she shot me down: "Well, I'm not talking about you, am I?" When I got home, I asked my mom for the name of my tribe and it was the same tribe my friend held in contempt! I had to sit with that. This girl who is supposed to be my friend hates me because of something I have no control over. She hates me because of my tribe, of all things. It's hard enough fitting in as a kid without adding an insecurity about lineage.

Tribalism is what propelled me to learn more about the war. Heated discussions of this tribe or another and pinpointing the real cause of the Civil War felt like a regular occurrence. I discovered over time that people are really prejudiced. Each group would pin the war entirely on another group, without batting an eye. Everyone believed their version of details with immovable conviction. These were the stories they heard from their parents and their parents before them. But if each side claimed a different account, who was right? And who was responsible for teaching us the full, unbiased account of the Civil War?

A part of my naivete was a sentiment for the ideal of Soomaalinimo. I trusted that despite whatever differences we had, there was a shared commonality among Somali people. We are bound through language, religion, food, culture, and everything in between. Sure, we had various tribes, classes, and other differences, but at the end of the day, we were Somali. But I soon realized that we did not all share this sentiment. That we were irreparably ruptured, and the lines had been drawn. I was indignant when I began to see those now obvious divisions that were always present. I started wondering, *Where did this come from, and why does everyone feel so strongly? And why didn't anyone tell me about it? Why didn't I know?* I felt I had been misguided on the true state of our Somali identity. As if someone didn't tell me the punch line to a really funny joke. I was left frustrated. Soomaalinimo is simply a façade, because we are so different culturally. We have some similar experiences, like being immigrants, and many of us are working class. But we're still different; to box in our experiences as the "Somali experience" is just not the full truth.

Over the years, I heard my fair share of over-the-top irrational prejudice against my tribe and other tribes. Kids at my school would joke that X-tribe would go to hell. One of my babysitters found out about our tribe and spread it at my masjid. We were immediately treated differently by kids and adults alike. I went to sit with my friends, and a girl stopped me and said, "You can only sit here if you're Majeerteen." We weren't welcome anymore. A friend of mine told me that X-tribe people are not even real Somalis. That in fact our lineage is mixed with other Africans and not pure Somali. Where did this come from? It was untrue, of course, but still, why would somebody believe that and why did it matter?

College was no different. I started getting active on social media and could not believe my eyes. Tribalism was rampant on sites like Twitter. Kids who had never set foot in an airport were proudly banging their chests about whose tribe was best and who they wouldn't be caught dead marrying. Many of these same kids didn't see the Civil War or could not string together three sentences in Somali, and yet were ardent tribalists. How? Why? To a large degree, they were separated from tribalism but chose to actively inherit it. It's something I still don't fully understand and perhaps never will. In one college class, a professor asked a group of us if a caste system existed in Somalia, and if so, which tribe was at the bottom. My classmates confidently answered X-tribe, despite the fact that my tribe is large and well known. They couldn't be serious, could they? I gathered myself before rushing to correct them, but they dug in their heels and insisted they were right. It was as if we existed in parallel universes, because there was simply no way that we operated from the same reality.

I realized that a large number of us don't know Somali history. Everything we know is from our parents and families, and those stories inevitably slant toward the tribes we claim. We aren't taught objective, neutral documentation of history; instead, we inherit war stories that pit us against one another as victors or victims, and sometimes both. If you don't know how little you know, it is not hard to hold prejudice against those you deem different or less than.

Social media was a place of great discovery and connection. I seldom related to the stories of Somali or tribe experience from my classmates and peers. I learned about Rahaweyn farmers who were looked down on for their way of life, or other Somalis who were discriminated against for not speaking Somali and weren't allowed to enroll in schools during Siad Barre's rule. I learned about Af-Maay, which some people don't recognize as a full language system that is similar to but distinct from af Soomaali. I asked a Sudanese friend why they have a tribe system but aren't as tribalistic as we are, and an answer evaded her. A friend of mine messaged me a picture that ruined my day. It was someone at the gun range with a weapon cocked, and the caption read, "One X-tribe down." I had a sick feeling in the pit of my stomach when I read it. I never ceased to be stunned by the abject hatred.

Still, I can't ignore the value of tribe systems when they work. To be able to trace your lineage hundreds of years back and know exactly where you came from without DNA tracing is somewhat rare in our modern world. Once my mother told me of a person who passed away alone, with no relatives or family. People soon learned of his subclan, and when word got out that he had died, everyone quickly assembled. The subclan raised the necessary funds for funeral costs and made sure the janazah was well attended. Many if not most of them had not met this person, but because they shared a clan, people made sure that he was taken care of, even in death. I would wager most people don't have that kind of community, so I recognize the blessings and beauty that can be produced from it. As with most things, it is what people make it to be. Tribe can be used for good or for evil—we ultimately decide how we want to operate.

As it is for most kids, college for me was a place of exploration and finding myself. I started out at a community college, and it was worlds removed from my university experience later on. In community college, everyone studied together. There was no racial or ethnic divide. I could walk past a table with random students from one class and immediately join them without reservation. It wasn't strange to randomly pop up and eat canjeero with a stranger studying the same subject. There was a real sense of camaraderie. Everyone wanted to help and be helped. We shared notes, lifted each other up, and encouraged each other to be our best. I studied chemistry with a Somali newcomer who was a whiz at math and science but was insecure about her English. She had been in the States for only a couple years, but she was far more advanced than us American-born kids in STEM.

University was a different experience, to put it mildly. At this school, people would rarely return salaam. The students were exclusive and cliquish. It wasn't enough to be ethnically or racially divided; there was separation down to ideology, upbringing, and a million more ways I couldn't begin to list. The students were unhelpful, hoarded resources, and didn't want others to win. I felt like I was on Mars without a space suit. I was not prepared for the atmosphere.

I had trouble figuring out the busing system, and no one offered to help or advise me. Basic things like that really magnified the differences between schools. I also walked into an expanding racial atomic bomb: the divide between Arab and Somali students. Arab students were racist toward Somalis, and stories would go around, like Arab students calling Somali kids loud and unruly in Arabic without realizing the number of Arabic-speaking Somalis. The irony was that some of these students were the children of racist masjid board members in a neighboring suburb who had escalated the dissolution of the masjid by calling Somalis cockroaches in between a Friday khutbah. The division extended beyond the kids; it reflected the community.

Those racial situations were the catalysts for my own reflections on race. For the first time, I had to investigate my Black identity. I didn't always identify with other Black people, because they rarely identified with us. In high school, our campus was rife with tension between Black Americans and Somalis. It heightened to the point where our principal had to sit us down and scold us: "You're all Black; what is your problem?" I did identify with other Africans. My identity was based on my ethnicity and religion first and foremost. In college, I began taking African studies courses. Some were very well done and well researched and helped shape my worldview. I was excited. Overall, I felt like I had found my people. Other people like me, trying to find out who we are and where we fit in this world. I joined student groups and lent my time to social causes. I found my tribe.

There was one class that always seemed to elicit roaring debate. Large groups of students took the class together and rolled in as friends and allies. The class was always tense, all members on pins and needles. It felt like everyone was waiting for some poor fool to make a mistake or say something slightly different in order to jump down their throats and denounce them. People didn't care about the required readings, and they weren't interested in constructive dialogue. Instead, everyone wanted to be right, all the time. They wanted the story of a battle to regale their friends or followers with, always exaggerated and without a modicum of self-awareness. Students came into the class with the baggage of their traumas or experiences and didn't shy away from projecting, generalizing, and breaking the basic rules of social agreements. Things like not assuming intention, giving others a chance to speak, and generally being kind. This class was a no-man's-land. Rule and order had no meaning here. It made for both an exciting and an exhausting hour.

Some classmates would painfully lie, in an agonizing attempt to gain the acceptance of others. They would minimize some aspects of themselves or exaggerate others to fit in. It felt strange and uncomfortable to witness, as if I had stumbled upon someone during a deeply personal and woeful circumstance. One classmate shared that perhaps because she was nontraditional and different from her parents and elders, she couldn't relate to her ethnic identity and instead felt closer to her idea of Black identity. The Black students in the class called her out and reminded her of her name, shared language, and culture. How could she not relate to something she so obviously was? With or without the acceptance or approval of her community, she remained who she was. So what warped her perception? Why do we force ourselves to conform to tiny boxes and then become bewildered when we don't quite fit? I realized then the fallacy and flaw of identity politics. I understood that people want to hide behind one identity. Why is it easier to cut yourself into pieces to become something than to simply be? It doesn't work, because it denies the complexity and nuance that comes with being human. What if any one person were reduced to a single identity? When are you a representative, and when are you an individual? Who appointed you?

I once did a bubble exercise in a room full of White people. We were asked, "Who are you?" I quickly got to work and jotted down all my identities: Black, Muslim, woman, and so forth. When I looked up, I saw everyone else had things like "hiker" and "reader." I felt so stupid. Why didn't I think about myself like that? I view myself in the context of America. I am an African Muslim woman in America. I wouldn't necessarily say I'm proud to be American, although I'm not ashamed either. I'm Somali, but I've found that this identity isn't as relevant as I once believed it to be—that is, I don't wear my ethnicity in the way I do my religion and skin color. That's what I relate to the most.

America loves identity. I have to be *othered*. I have to fit in a box, because this is how other people make sense of me. They know what to think of me—or rather, they know what assumptions to make. I am Muslim, Black, Somali, woman, daughter of immigrants, and working class. I am X, and I suffer from Y. But those marginalizations are not the core of who I am, and at times they are simply barriers to my success. Of course these identities are not inherently barriers at their core, but I may be treated with prejudice because of them.

I had to take a step back and realize how flawed my thinking was. I was disturbed to be wrong about Black identity the way I was wrong about Soomaalinimo or the "One Ummah" unity among Muslims. Yes, we share identities, but we are millions of individuals who make a collective. Still, we are individuals at our core, with unique experiences, ideas, and beliefs. I realized my "tribe" are the people who think like me, who share my mindset, not merely my skin color, tribe, race, ethnicity.

Identity politics has done a number on Somali kids and people in general. This worldview makes you more isolated and forces you to make yourself smaller, because you limit who you can be and who you can be in community with. It also makes you more suspicious and critical of the world. You become more ignorant. You think everybody is a prejudiced bigot and so on and so forth. It makes you paranoid. You constantly have to assess the judgments you're absolutely sure people are making against you. It reduces the humanity of others to a shallow calculation based on immutable traits as factors.

It is also narcissistic, because you recognize how complicated you are, with corresponding shades of gray, but insist that everyone else must be black and white. We are judged based on identity and not on the value of ideas or beliefs. You're constantly made to believe the world hates you, everyone must think you're stupid and ugly. If someone likes you, it must be a fetish, because who could find you attractive? You have to find microaggressions in every encounter, until the idea of interacting with X-group exhausts you. It's not hard to imagine what happens when you tell people that they have no one but themselves. You would feel very lonely, think everyone is prejudiced and that people are no longer human. They must know everything you do and choose to be wrong anyway out of spite. But ignorance is not intent.

It's really important for you to know your history, because it gives you context—but at the same time you are a mosaic of your own unique experiences and ideas, with your own future and destiny. One of my favorite passages in the Qur'an that gives me solace is when Illahi says, "O mankind! Lo! We have created you male and female, and have made you nations and tribes that ye may know one another. Lo! the noblest of you, in the sight of Allah, is the best in conduct. Lo! Allah is Knower, Aware" (Qur'an 49:13). It poetically demonstrates that differences are not division. We are not better than one another based on immutable traits, but instead are made distinct by our character and conduct. We have the free will to decide exactly the type of person we want to be. The Prophet Muhammad ﷺ warned us about this division and prejudice against others that can be interpreted as tribalism, nationalism, racism, and divisiveness. That arrogance is our lowest self. We must do everything in our power to not give into it.

For young Somalis dealing with identity issues, I empathize

with you. I grew up in the States the daughter of immigrants and had to deal with identity in a way that the adults in my life couldn't relate to. I think it is important for you to establish "What do you hold to be true?" For me, I go back to that ayah often. You need to develop a moral compass that can help you figure out what you believe. Issues, topics, current events change every day, but what are your core principles that you live by? What are you against? What do you stand for? What are you willing to die for? Spend time in introspection and examine who you are. Besides your labels, who are you actually? What do you think is right? What do you think is wrong? Look at people as individuals and treat them with the same understanding and respect you would want to be afforded. You have to constantly question things and do your own research. Not all education is good education. For me, going to college was like taking a philosophy course: I walked away knowing less than I did before. Academia is straight indoctrination. We are conditioned to run with little information. Everyone's an expert. It's about clout, views, and money. There's no credibility or fact-checking. Listen to your gut and common sense. Everyone is pushing their own personal agenda.

Islam has always kept me grounded, despite being pushed out of two masjids, one for tribalism and one for racism. Those experiences never affected my relationship to Islam and with Allah (سبحانه وتعالى). It served as a protection to me. When I don't have the answers, I can look to my diin and find it. There are of course Muslim people who are prejudiced or racist, but that doesn't reflect Islam; it reflects them as people. We are not infallible, nor were we intended to be. I find it odd that some people hold shayukh to an extremely rigid and high standard but will carry water for feminists and liberals who are problematic. When either of those groups says the most racist or offensive thing, there is no shortage of excuses or passes. I have confidence and faith in my diin. If I find a shaykh I don't connect with or see myself in a spiritual alignment with, I just stick to the shayukh I can take from. It's no skin off my back.

Islam cannot be reduced to a label. Even though I was born into it, it's one of the few things I chose. Community is an important part of my faith, but Islam doesn't rely on people to make it. Islam is my way of life and my compass. It's not just something I am. My relationship with Allah (سبحانه وتعالى) transcends this world! Islam is the one thing I know is real. If it wasn't for Islam, I would be confused. I wouldn't know my right from my left. If I was told one day, "No *that's* your right, and that's really your left," I woulda been like, "Oh, word? That's my right?" The most important thing about my relationship to Allah (سبحانه وتعالى) is His forgiveness and acceptance. It's the one thing that does not make you sad. You no longer feel alone.

～

My first real job was at a substance abuse treatment center. I was looking for a job to make some money, and a friend hooked me up. I worked at a family treatment center with moms and their kids, pregnant women, or women trying to get their kids back from the authorities. I was a home lead, so I passed out medications or administered them. I worked overnight. Night shift made sense, because I made more money and it wasn't as busy as daytime. It was my first mental health job. The profession is exhausting. They don't prepare you for what you will see and hear. You can get secondhand trauma. In an office setting, having a lazy coworker is something that hurts people's pockets. But in health care, a lazy or irresponsible coworker dealing with patients can hurt people in real life. Diligence is key.

I stayed at the facility for a long time. I was in college working toward the medical field. The day-to-day consisted of transporting clients or helping transport their kids to day care. I interacted with a lot of people and saw up close the system that leads people to addiction. Some were prostitutes, some had addiction in their family, a history of domestic abuse, DUIs, house arrest, and so on and so forth. I started seeing the patterns over and over again. Some people were stuck in an endless loop, coming back again and again and again. Addiction was just one aspect of their life. They also had bipolar disorder, depression, and PTSD. I realized they were set up for failure before they even left our facility. They didn't have housing, so they were placed in a homeless shelter or sent back to the place where they became addicted or had access to drugs. What would happen when they inevitably messed up? My eyes were opened to how broken the health care system is. Mental health is not 100 percent clinical; a lot of it has to do with your environment. And we were sending people into the lion's den.

The facility would indiscriminately hire people who applied, without care for motivations or goals. They didn't try to retain valuable staff. There was one woman who already had money but worked there because she genuinely cared about the patients. It wasn't about a paycheck to her. She was fired because she didn't follow all the rules and bow down to management.

I also saw how the police interacted with these women—and rules in general. The thing about cops is, whether or not something is the law, they know they are the authorities and can do what they want. When I was at the substance center, the cops had warrants for patients' arrests. By law, we did not have to let them in or tell them about patients, but they would threaten staff with arrest. They did not care about the law because they instead believed themselves to be the physical manifestation of the law; they were the law.

I ended up leaving the job because of racism. I was helping a patient with a fairly routine task. One White supervisor began yelling at me in front of the patient for doing it wrong. I explained that I had done the task many times before and was very confident I was following procedure. She was furious. She ended up going to a supervisor meeting and said I was disrespectful and raised my voice at her, which made me look aggressive and out of control. The only Black supervisor and a solid woman backed me up and said, "I know her; that doesn't sound like her at all." It was the straw that broke the camel's back. I was gone soon after.

My next job was in a mental health ward at a large hospital. My friends were psych associates and often talked about their interesting jobs. They talked about working in teams with doctors and nurses and with patients. I wanted to go into health care, so it made sense. Just like with the treatment center, I was not properly prepared for this role. I wasn't ready to work in a mental health unit with such high-acuity patients. We did a month of training to get ready, but we were not really learning about psych and mental health disorders. The training focused on terminology, but it's so much more than that. You don't really know until you start working with patients. You have to work with someone who has low-functioning autism, TBI, or fetal alcohol syndrome to really understand how to work with them.

It also felt like glorified babysitting. We had to prevent patients from hurting themselves and other people. We do rounds, we cover other people's breaks, and you have a number of patients you check in with on any given shift. Sometimes we do a one-to-one: you stay with one patient the whole time. You get two breaks and that's it. You are that person's shadow. It is so exhausting and draining. And you might not have the ability to work with people. The shifts run the gamut of being tedious or terrifying. You might get someone threatening to kill their parents, or a patient who is catatonic, or someone with schizophrenia who has hallucinations, or a suicidal nineteen-year-old struggling with abuse. Having a huge mix or varied scale of patients means some of them will be neglected.

I also learned quickly how racist the hospital was and how genuinely unprepared they are to deal with POC but especially Somali patients. Even though Somalis are a small percentage of the population, we regularly saw many Somali patients. So much so that it made no sense that the hospital did not have clear guidelines, support, or a system for caring for Somali patients, a number of whom did not speak English. I have friends who work in other hospitals, but we all agreed this one was the worst offender. The staff here didn't bother to learn the names of their Somali patients. Names like Ali or Abdi were simply impossible to recall. We once had an old Somali man checked in who was not eating food or taking care of himself. He was tagged as a danger to himself. But there was not much they could do for him—or did do, for that matter. I would walk into his room for the night shift and his uneaten breakfast was still there, the sheets unchanged and rumpled, the room a mess. He was not in immediate danger to anyone, but he has his dignity. The hospital staff should have treated him with a measure of respect. It's our job to care for our patients; it's quite literally the least we can do. Public health staff did COVID response outreach for Somali patients, but where were they before? That might be the only example of outreach they've done to Somali patients, in 2020 no less!

I had one doctor pull me out of a task once to interpret for a patient. I said, "Let me go see if there is an interpreter in the building." He waved me off in complete disdain. I left to go find an interpreter, and when I got back, the doctor was gone. He had seen the patient without an interpreter and just winged it. I just shook my head. The recklessness of it all. One of my biggest pet peeves is being pulled from a patient to be asked to interpret. I have no problem interpreting for anyone who asks; I've interpreted many times in non-medical roles. I am simply unqualified to interpret in medical situations. I've not been trained on terminology or other things I need to know. I could assume a great deal of risk interpreting for something with such high stakes.

The interpreting situations illuminate how much of an afterthought non-English-speaking or Somali patients are to the hospital. Medical providers know at least one day prior which patients they examine, and their charts will say if they need an interpreter or not, but the providers insist on being unprepared. One time during a holiday they told me, "There's no interpreter during the holiday; can you come talk to a patient?" I resigned myself to interpret. If I hadn't done it, they wouldn't use a phone call interpreter; they just worked with the little English she knew. They could barely understand each other. How could they think this was acceptable?

There were all different kinds of Somalis in the ward. Kids that grew up here or back home, teenagers, elderly, and everyone in between. Our Somali patients would be a lot more acute than others. They would not want to work with Somali staff. They may have been scared we would judge them, or maybe they were embarrassed by the stigma of mental health. Some saw people killed back home during the war. There was a lot of trauma in the ward. Some were held by ICE for a few months before being placed. I'll never forget one woman. The nurse tried to take her temperature during a routine exam, and she flinched hard. I was interpreting and asked why she flinched, and she said she thought the nurse was gonna hit her. I was heartbroken for her. What had she seen?

The mental health units didn't have any Somali nurses. Our community has many skilled and talented nurses, so why didn't our units have any? The other staff were also woefully ignorant about Somali culture. For example, one older Somali man often spoke loudly and used his hands to speak, but he wasn't angry. He just spoke expressively. But they don't understand the culture: they saw a Somali being loud and categorized that as aggressive. During Ramadan, they would do music therapy for patients. A Muslim kid didn't want to be there, and they couldn't understand why. Many musical instruments are haraam, and listening to it would break your fast. They placed the Qur'an with other books, and people would obviously touch it and move it and stack other books on top of it. It frustrated one patient to no end. I would move the kitabs. Another kid wanted to purify himself so he could pray, but showers are only available from 7:00 AM to 10:00 PM. Staff members found me and asked if what he was asking for was a real thing in our culture. I said yes, and they let him shower. Had I not been there and confirmed that, he could've flipped out and thrown things at them.

Black patients, and especially Black males, were viewed with suspicion of aggression. One patient was placed in an observation unit, a room made to handle hostile and violent patients. The room was within another room, with a 24/7 surveillance camera and plexiglass on all sides of the inner room. Patients have a bathroom, and meals are delivered to them. Only one patient is in there at a time, and they cannot come out. This patient was in observation for weeks, but he did not need it. Patients have a TV and other items but very limited interaction with others. He was becoming more and more depressed. A nurse filed a complaint because she did not know why he was in there for so long. To make matters worse, he didn't see his provider regularly. To be clear, all patients in our units see their providers every day, except for weekends and holidays. Apparently his provider, who placed him there, said she was too afraid of him. He was behind plexiglass; he couldn't even get to her. He had also allegedly threatened her. In our field, patients threaten us all the time. That's the job. They even harm you sometimes, but that can happen when you're working with these types of patients. But this man was not a threat to himself or other people. The Black people who worked there knew he was there because he was Black. There was no permissible reason for essentially placing him in indefinite solitary confinement.

What the general public doesn't understand about mental health is that it can also be used to get away with bad behavior. There are people who know how to game the system. They know what to say to whom, how to act, and what they can get away with. We had one woman who was very difficult. She was always in trouble for something, but always managed to get away scot-free. She was afforded massive advantages that other patients couldn't dream of. She would intentionally harm staff and other patients, but was not moved or arrested. She knew what to say and to whom in order to be viewed as a passive victim and not the aggressor she typically was.

There was another patient I was told to stay away from at all costs. We later found out he was admitted for committing a physical hate crime against a Somali person. It was a violent crime, but he did not have to do any time. There are Somali boys in this state serving sentences of thirty years or more for conspiracy. And then there are others: the feds find mentally ill people who get close to committing a crime, entrap these people, solve their own case, and give each other pats on the back. The only difference between those mental illnesses is that one serves an agenda and the other doesn't. If you're the right type of person, the court might give you a slap on the wrist. If you're the wrong type of person, they'll make an example out of you.

～

My hijab story and perspective is not something I see often. In fact, it's something I rarely hear about. I usually hear one of two things from other girls. It's either "I was forced" or "I discovered it was the most beautiful thing." I had a different relationship with hijab. I grew up in the masjid where everyone wore hijab. My mom wore hijab as well, and I wanted to be like her, a sophisticated adult. It felt like the natural course. When I initially put it on, I thought I could switch between hijab and khamaar. My mom would see me in a khamaar and say, "My goodness, you're naked! What are you wearing? Once you wear a hijab, you can't just take it off."

At dugsi, our macalamiin would say to us, "If you don't wear a jilbaab, that's not hijab." I felt pressure from all corners. One day, a girl who was new to the masjid and perhaps new to Minnesota casually walked into our class. She was curious about our studies and had been chatting it up with other girls in the hallway. Our macalin kicked her out because she had on an abaya and khamaar. "I don't want to see her like this; she shouldn't be wearing that in this class." I felt bad for her. Learning Islamic studies is not as accessible as people say it is. Once I started wearing hijab, it was no longer a choice. It was no longer something I wanted.

Jilbaab also ostracized me from other peers. I didn't find my tribe in high school. A girl I knew would transform from jilbaab to khamaar on the bus route. People will see the jilbaab and think, "Oh, she's a goody two-shoes, she's religious, she can't relate to us." I hung out with all sorts of people. Girls my age and who were born here wore khamaar, so I stuck out like a sore thumb. People would think I'm a FOB for wearing a jilbaab and then be surprised to find out I wasn't.

It wasn't just Somalis; wearing jilbaab or any hijab for that matter also alienated me from my White classmates. I was walking down the hallway one day when a mixed classmate said, "She looks like a terrorist." It was definitely rude, but having my appearance ostracize me from my Muslim peers mattered more than White kids being racist. Other Somali girls didn't know I didn't have a choice in the matter.

At the same time, some of my behaviors were off-putting to those girls. One time a girl pressed me on the bus, asking, "Why do you sit with FOBs? What do you have in common?" She genuinely detested them. It didn't make sense to me, because if you think about it, our moms are FOBs. Even though you're different in many ways, why outright hate a group of people? It's a social class thing. Her underlying question was, why are you subjecting yourself to this lifestyle? Because being a part of one group meant that you were not a part of the other group. But I didn't fit in anywhere. So what difference did it make?

Wearing a jilbaab, I felt like I had to live up to the religious label. I can't do this, can't mess up here, can't act like this, gotta react like that. I even had to control the way I behaved around friends. My inner thoughts would say, *They expect you to say this.* It was a lot of pressure to live up to.

Then I went to college. I got a job; I started having money and, pretty soon, my own car. My life had agency now. I felt like I was in charge for the first time. It became even harder to wear jilbaab. In Islam, there is no compulsion. But as Muslims, there's a great deal of pressure. The pressure was bubbling up inside of me, looking for release. I started having conversations with my mom about hijab. I started switching off between hijab and khamaar. Then one day my mom said, "You keep bringing up khamaar; why don't you just wear it?" After that, I put on a khamaar and never took it off. I had a bad relationship with jilbaab and didn't choose it. I no longer lived without agency.

It was only after I let jilbaab go that I truly started to appreciate hijab and jilbaab. I always heard, "Hijab is a protection." I believed in it in an abstract sense, but never really appreciated it. When I started wearing khamaar full-time, it came with a whole new territory. What size am I? What shirt fits right? What sticks out? What looks good? I went to a popular fast fashion store and had an almost out-of-body experience. I grabbed a bunch of things off a rack and went to try them on. I started thinking, *My proportions are different. Am I really this size? Why does this part of my body look like that?* I had a near breakdown in a dressing room. It felt like I was looking at my body for the first time ever. I was caught completely off guard because I never had thought like that before. I never thought that deeply about my body and the way it looks. I realized then that donning a khamaar came with its own set of problems. It came with having to acknowledge societal ideals about women's bodies. It came with doubt and shame about things I had never given a moment's thought before. It came with body image and comparing yourself to other women. It came with acknowledging desirability, sexualization, and an insecurity about the way I looked and how I measured up. I used to usually wear abaya and jilbaab. With abaya, all you need to know is your height. The bust, waist, and hips were one-size-fits-all. My clothes were loose-fitting, and I never had to pay attention to the body underneath.

When I started wearing khamaar, I started getting all kinds of comments on my body. People would congratulate me for a job well done on losing weight, and I would think, *What weight did I lose?* I cannot say if I truly was chubby, but it illustrates how detached I was from body image issues. What if I had seen myself the way they had seen me? Would I have spent my adolescence or teenage years obsessed with my body? Examining every inch for something to pinch and prod? Constantly in a mirror looking for a flaw to cry about or something to be proud of? I was not satisfied or dissatisfied with my body; I was simply oblivious. In hindsight, I came to appreciate hijab for how it protected me from society and myself.

〜

To Somali people, I pray that we one day end the ignorance and divisiveness. Take it upon yourself to learn your history and learn from the error of our ways.

To Somali boys, you have a lot of pressure on you. And I wish that you could share that and not compare yourself to Somali girls or your sisters, share that and open up to us. We are a resource, not competition. We have a lot more in common than we differ. Reach out if you need advice or if you feel alone.

To Somali girls, you are under a lot of pressure; I compare it to Black excellence. You have to excel and work ten times harder. Get your master's, get a career, get married in your twenties and have kids, have fabulous lives on Instagram, leave a legacy for your family, be the first to do this or that, uplift your family from poverty, break generational cycles, and so on. When we put it all together, it is not realistic or healthy to expect one person to do all this. Take a step back and put it all into perspective. If you are in a better place than your parents were, that is a success! Be enough. If your parents brought you here and you're dealing with the same burdens or issues they had, then all the money and success in the world could not hide that we haven't gotten anywhere. If you can say, "Me and my mom have a healthy relationship, and she and her mother did not," that is a huge success.

Break out of cycles, take risks—that's success. Somali women are so scared of not going into a traditional career or not going a traditional route. Success is having the guts to go your own way.

3

Warsan Omar, 20s, Mombasa, Kenya

pseudonym

I was born in Mombasa, Kenya. My family came to the States very early in my life. I barely remember life before America; Minnesota is home to me, and it's all I've ever really known. For the most part, I went to the same schools and grew up in a suburb all the way through high school. I'm now a university student.

I'm a middle child in a household of ten kids. I'm number five, smack-dab in the middle. I have a sister who passed away, God have mercy on her. I was blessed to be raised by both parents. My name, Warsan, means companion or friend. I love my name. I was named after my mom's sister. People tell me all the time we look alike; perhaps that's why I was named after her.

When we came to the States, I was wrongly placed in second grade. After a while, my teachers figured out I had no idea what was going on in the classroom and put me in first grade. I was taught English during my short time in school in Kenya. My older siblings were told they carried British accents because that's how we were taught in Mombasa. English wasn't hard for me to pick up at all. Despite that, I was placed in ESL. I didn't mind because my friends were in the class. It's where we went to goof off, have fun, and hang out. But by middle school, I couldn't help but think, *Why am I still here?* Still, I stuck around. It wasn't until I got my outstanding results for the state standardized tests that I was placed out. In hindsight, I didn't need to be there for as long as I was, but I didn't know how to advocate for myself and my parents thought it was just another helpful class. It wasn't bad at first, but at some point it got so easy, it felt comical.

In junior high, we had an after-school community center. If your parents worked late or you wanted to hang out, you could go to the center. It had games and toys, and it was right next to our school. I remember my mom always saying I couldn't go. I felt left out from my friends. My mom couldn't drive at the time, and my dad would usually be working with the one car we shared as a family. She didn't want to take any risks from me walking home by myself because anything could happen. If it wasn't school related, it wasn't seen as important by my parents.

Growing up, I had very supportive teachers. They would always offer their help and never made me feel like an outcast because I was different. My high school counselor, on the other hand, was my nemesis. She was never outwardly mean or aggressive toward me. Instead, she just politely slowed me down and doubted me during my time at the school. She didn't think I was capable of getting accepted to Augsburg—or any college, for that matter. I was saddened that I didn't have a good relationship with her, couldn't go to her for help on an application or to get advice. It bothered me because I saw that a lot of my White classmates did have that relationship with her. It made me question myself. Was I doing something wrong? Should I be nicer to her? Is it me? After a while, I gave up trying to get on her good side.

Applications were soon due for colleges, and we had to apply on an app through our school counselor. Every time I would ask her to look at an application or review a document, she would say, "I have a lot to do; I'll try to get to it, but I don't know." I said screw it and applied to every school, one at a time, by myself. I knew she was holding me back, and I wasn't going to let her get in my way. If I waited on her, I don't know if I would've made the application deadlines. At first, I thought I was the only one. But then I found out she didn't have good relationships with a few other Somali girls, and I started to connect the dots. I felt relieved to know it wasn't me; it was her. I had been in a college readiness program called College Possible since seventh grade. I started going to them for help on how to do things for college acceptance instead. I was accepted into Augsburg [in Minneapolis], where I'm studying now.

I was the only Somali or hijabi for most of my time in school. I remember having to explain to my classmates that I didn't celebrate Christmas and that I observed fast during Ramadan. "Aren't you going to die?" I heard this question every year and resigned myself to explaining for eternity. I knew early on I was not quite like my White classmates. I am a Black Muslim Somali girl. By seventh grade, more minorities were attending our school district. By high school, the racism had gotten considerably worse. The school demographics were changing, and tensions were rising.

One time, a group of younger girls were sitting in the cafeteria and, out of nowhere, a White boy started throwing carrots at them. They got mad at him and started yelling at him, and an argument ensued. When they told me what happened, I said we need to go straight to the principal, forget the counselors. "This is crazy." We went to the principal's office, and he brought in an SRO and chided us: "You know, there are other ways of handling things." Everyone there was White except the other East African Muslim girls. How could the school staff relate to being picked on for the color of your skin or your religion? We would get cussed out or have things thrown at us, and then get blamed for reacting or defending ourselves. They wanted us to allow ourselves to be bullied. Then the police officer said she understood how we felt because "I too get bullied every day for wearing this badge." This woman compared her job to us being discriminated against on the basis of race or religion. We knew these people couldn't have our backs. I was so angry at that point. Here we were being bullied and the adults who were supposed to protect us were telling us not to fight back, to take it. And the bullies just got away with it. It was such a disheartening thing to experience at an age when and a place where our power was limited.

As a college student, I'm reminded of how grateful I am to the first Somali students on college campuses who broke barriers for us years ago. Now when I go to the campus, there are so many Somali students. It must have been much harder earlier on, when we first started immigrating to Minnesota. Lucky for me, I have two college-age neighbors who helped me navigate Augsburg when I first got to college. I'm indebted to them for their help.

I am currently studying health service management. I've always wanted to help people. I'm also a people person. I enjoy talking to others and getting to know them. This field is the right match for me. My dream is to open my own hospital or clinic one day. I would be very attentive to and protective of Black women and make sure they received top-of-the-line care. Safety, trust, and comfort would be my priorities. Health care in the States is so profit-driven. It's completely void of a principled focus on health and wellness. It's a huge industry and a money trap. Some people go into health care or government wanting to make change, and they end up becoming what they were fighting against. In the health care field, there's a need for humility and empathy. For example, the cost of insulin is a barrier to many people, but they need it to live. People are dying from not having it. It's unethical and hard to believe that this is a modern problem that happens in the richest country in the world.

In our community, we have our share of health issues. The standard Somali diet now resembles the standard American diet, which is not good for our health. We have problems with diabetes, high blood pressure, thyroid conditions, heart conditions—and a lot of it is tied to diet and exercise. It's important for us to move our bodies and take care of ourselves. Somali moms love the YMCA and working out. They love sharing health tips or going for walks. The desire is there; how do we make it easier for our community? Jilbaab and loose clothing can be a hazard in a gym. Imagine if we had women-only gyms or health centers. For men, it's easy to exercise wherever and whenever. But Muslim women have to consciously think about where they can go that has privacy, safety, etc. We need to build those spaces for our communities here as well. I have a dream of doing something in health care systems back home, once I get educated and build myself professionally in the States. I would work with the local doctors and medical professionals on solutions, not just do something on my own.

∼

Both of my parents are from Kismaayo. Dad works at a medical device company. Mom recently started working at Amazon. I told my mom not to work there because I was worried about Islamophobia or bigotry she might endure. I didn't want her to work there because I didn't want her supervisors or coworkers to be mean to her. She speaks English but not fluently. I was afraid other people would mistreat her. And I didn't like Amazon because they have issues with Muslims taking prayer breaks. I read on social media about how they mistreat all their employees with few or no breaks, quotas, and just an inhumane work environment. I really didn't want her to work there. But then I found out a lot of Somali moms work there, and I felt a lot more comfortable. She made friends, and people look out for each other. At the end of the day, she can help provide, and that's what matters.

My parents don't really talk about their pasts. My mom never got a chance to go to school or dugsi because she lived in rural places. Her role, and my uncle's, was to help my grandma. So Mom didn't get that opportunity for education. My maternal grandma is my only living grandparent, and she's in Kenya.

My relationship with my dad is pretty casual. He's barely home because he works. We don't really talk. He's always tired. I can ask him for money if I need it, and that's pretty much it. I wish I could get advice from him and confide in him. But you just stop trying after a while. I've tried to build a more meaningful relationship, but it doesn't go anywhere. After a certain point, it just feels like a waste of time. He has a better relationship with my youngest sibling because he's little and my dad spoils him. My oldest brother has a better relationship with him too. It's not a super strong relationship, but it's decent compared to the rest of us.

My parents are super serious about education. Especially my mom, because she didn't get the chance, so we can't fumble it. They expect us to go to college, get a master's, make a living. Our parents brought us here for a better life. When I was a kid, I didn't think citizenship was a big deal. I remember my mom listening to cassette tapes, practicing for the citizenship test. She would constantly replay the tapes. It was so annoying; I don't know how many times I've heard the preamble to the Constitution. My mom would ask me to quiz her any chance she got. And then as I got older, I realized being a citizen means you can live comfortably. For my parents, citizenship means stability and comfort. My parents were elated to become citizens. It meant their dreams were coming true.

My mom didn't know how to read or write English. She's a very smart woman, but she didn't have the opportunity for education like my dad did. My dad knows how to read, write, and speak English well. It was harder for my mom to study for the test. So, later in life, my mom went to ELL classes and worked really hard to learn how to read and write. She worked very hard to be able to take the citizenship test. It was a huge accomplishment for her to pass the test. She passed on her first try. She was so happy, and we were all proud of her. I'm sure she'll never forget those citizenship questions.

The Muslim ban and the Trump administration made me think more about citizenship. I have an awareness of the world that exists beyond this country, and that's something that is absent in the minds of most Americans. I remember the poet Warsan Shire said in her work that nobody leaves home unless home is consuming you. No one wants to leave their home, but people don't have a choice in the matter. It's about acknowledging the humanity in others. When you can't do that, you're in trouble. In the West, it's very easy to detach yourself from the existence of other people. It's a very greedy and selfish way to live. You can take, take, take, but you can't help others when they need it? What kind of life is that?

As a middle child, I am often forgotten. Not in a malicious way but just because I'm grown and I don't give my parents anything to worry about. They have the little kids to worry about and my older brothers but not me.

My parents aren't affectionate. They don't hug and kiss us and say, "I love you." My mom every once in a while might say, "I love you," but that's pretty much it. I know they're proud of us; maybe that's how they show love. I would love a better relationship with my mom. It's not bad; it's just basic. I don't get one-on-one time with either of my parents. My parents provide for us; we get everything we need. But emotionally, it's lacking. I can't tell my parents if I'm going through something because they would belittle it. Like friendship problems. I wish I could talk to my parents about anything, but I know I can't really do that. I wish we could hang out and be around each other. I wish we were closer.

I wish my parents put more effort into making us feel connected as a family. Sometimes it just feels like people who happen to live together instead of a family unit. I wish I could change it, but it's not up to me. My parents set the standard. In the past, I definitely made an effort to change things, and when it didn't work, I was saddened. But I had to come to terms with knowing that there was nothing I could do to fill that gap with my family. I could only promise to do things differently when I have a family of my own.

Our parents don't know how to apologize to us or admit their mistakes. I remember one time I got in an argument with my mom and it was something that she did wrong. And I told my dad about it, and he's like, "That's your mom. You need to apologize to her." That made no sense to me.

What I learned about Somali culture through my parents was by watching, not listening, because my parents didn't sit us down like that. Art was not highlighted. But roles and rules were. Like keeping the family close, what is a part of our diin and what isn't.

Growing up, I hated how strict my parents were with my sisters and me, while they were so easygoing with my brothers. I started cleaning around fifth or sixth grade. Cleaning and cooking are absolutely necessary life skills; I have no problem doing them. The issue for me was cleaning up after grown men. Do they not have hands? The unfairness just creates resentment and anger. If I asked about why they didn't help out around the house, I was told to mind my business. It was so frustrating. They were just as capable. And they were smug about it. Like they had one up on me because I'm a girl. They laughed about it. Like during Ramadan when everybody was finished eating, my mom would tell us, "Go do the dishes." And my brothers would just start laughing. They'll be like, "I don't need to do the dishes.

I'm a guy." You just get frustrated because it's annoying. We're literally around the same age. But there's nothing you can do. It bothers you, but you have to get on with it.

My relationships with my siblings vary. If I need anything, I can ask my older brother. We don't have much in common besides that. It's weird, because I really don't have a strong relationship with any of my siblings either, except perhaps for my youngest brother. I remember when he was born, taking care of him and playing with him. I'm very overprotective of him. I don't want him to adopt my other brothers' attitude toward domestic things. My little brother is shy and polite; he really keeps to himself. So I let him know I'm there for him emotionally, in a way my parents weren't for me. He can tell me anything. Same for my sisters.

My oldest sister and I have had a really tumultuous relationship. We're only a couple years apart, but I'm not close to her because of the negative things she's done to me. We're not on speaking terms right now. We've been like that for three years. It just got to a breaking point for me, and I decided that I didn't want anything to do with her. When I first told my mom about our situation, she thought I was joking. After six months my mom said, "Talk to her. What's the point of this?" Before that, we would constantly argue and there was animosity between us. Despite this, I hope neither of us leaves this earth before we resolve our issues, because that would be heartbreaking. We don't have to reconcile, but I want there to be forgiveness so we don't have animosity for each other.

Despite life's challenges, I'm most grateful I grew up in a home with both my parents. The trauma of an absent parent is immeasurable and something I'm grateful I did not have to experience.

〜

I remember the first time I got on social media. I made a Facebook account in the sixth grade. I was not allowed to have an account, so I had to sneak around with it. One day, I forgot to log out on our home computer, and my mom found it and made me delete the account. Then I got an iPod and got Snapchat, and then Instagram. I was in the eighth grade when I started that. I used social media for entertainment and to talk to my friends. I mostly got my news from Twitter because kids my age don't really watch the news. Social media has its pros: entertainment, making friends, being connected, and expressing yourself. But it can be toxic. You can become addicted to attention through likes and follows. It can control you and consume you. Twitter can be terrible, especially when people use it to attack or publicly humiliate others. I remember seeing kids argue with each other in school and end up exposing each other online. Or there would be drama over social media, and everybody would just watch like it was a big spectacle. Twitter drama entertains people. Sure, it could be a joke for you because you're not involved, but for the subject of the drama, it's probably something they're thinking about every day. I always saw it from that perspective. I had a friend who was bullied so bad she switched schools. Sometimes you just have to get away from it.

Social media is really draining. My generation uses it as a news source now because we're not on CNN or Fox News. We get a lot of information from Twitter. But it's so overwhelming hearing and seeing the injustices happening all over the world. We see videos about what is happening to the Muslims in China, and it's heartbreaking. I cannot bring myself to watch those videos. How is that not supposed to affect you? It drives me crazy. We see police killing unarmed Black people and walking away free. There's a guilt you feel witnessing it and at the same time being helpless to stop it.

I remember when I first saw news of the Christchurch massacre, and I couldn't believe what had happened. I was asleep at home and woke up and checked Twitter. This was during Ramadan. And I was sick to my stomach. I knew that someday Islamophobia would drive people to do something evil, but it was another thing entirely seeing the faces of the victims that man killed. I knew how much some people hate Muslims, especially in the West, but to shoot up a masjid during Friday prayer? This was next-level evil. Because of the time zones, we had not had Friday prayer yet in America. People were talking about canceling Friday prayer or being scared to go pray. But we filled out the masjids anyway. In Islam we have this concept of trust in God. Yes, you're scared, but you have to have faith. We trust bus drivers, Uber drivers, and pilots to get us to our destination, so why shouldn't we trust the Almighty Creator to be in control of our destination? It's something I am still working on, but it's very important for me to allow Allah (سبحانه وتعالى) to handle things and not allow fear to control me.

I would love to go back home one day. My dream is to open a health clinic. But I have to be careful because I feel like it's easy to fall into a trap. We shouldn't see ourselves as saviors, just because of our education and resources. At the same time, we should not completely disconnect ourselves from our people and think only of our immediate family and jobs. It's only by the grace of God that we are here and have the opportunities we have. Let's be humble and then do what we can to make our country better. We should go back to help, not to exploit or be saviors.

∼

Sometimes people will argue with Somalis about being Black because they think East Africans are not Black. They think we're descended from Arabs or that our features are like Europeans'. All life started from East Africa: how are we European? We have every type of feature known to humankind because the world came from us. I do think being Muslim is the reason we're singled out, as opposed to Kenyans or Ethiopians. People associate Muslims with Arabs and don't understand that Islam is our faith, not a race or ethnicity. I don't even entertain that nonsense. People have such misinformed ideas on race. I think it has to do with our education on race. In school, we barely learned about Black history. Our teachers would cover the civil rights movement and slavery and that's about it. Our world history classes would be about Western nations. I felt like there were entire corners of the earth we are simply uneducated on. It wasn't until I sought out that knowledge myself that I learned more about Black history and African history. It's such an important thing to understand and such a wide field to study that it's a disservice to students to not teach it in schools.

It almost seems like if you grow up here or if you were raised here, this idea of race is unconsciously informed all the time. When we were in an African country, it's not something that you were ever really consciously or even unconsciously faced with. But here, you're always reminded.

~

There is a generational divide in our community. None of us relate to each other because now we're all growing up in different times and circumstances. Older people will freak out about the youth, but the thing is that there will always be a younger generation. The youth are the youth. Young people will always do things that aren't good for them, they will be rebellious, and they'll make mistakes. That's the price of being young. But do older people go out of their way to emotionally understand their child? I'm not sure. I think some parents are having kids on cruise control; that is to say, they aren't mentally prepared for being a parent. We've been through a lot as a people. War, refugee camps, coming to a whole new environment. There's so much unacknowledged trauma that we are passing down unintentionally. But that's why we need to interrupt that cycle.

Qabil is something that is not a big deal to me or my generation. My parents taught us our abtiris and wanted us to know that part of our history. If we mentioned so-and-so tribe in conversation, my parents would be like, "What? Who taught you that?" They were not big on tribe. In school or on social media, qabil is one big joke. There are memes on such-and-such qabil, and people just joke about it in a fake-superior way. Maybe we shouldn't, though, because we didn't heal the tribalism that has helped put our country the way it is now.

I love how Somali people are the funniest people in the world. We inherited humor. No matter where we live now, Somali people just find the humor of life and crack jokes about anything. We also love chai tea from Starbucks. It's a waste of money, but we're obsessed.

Somalia is home. An unspoken home. In a way, it's always felt like home because I have more ties there than anywhere else. Minnesota is all I know, so logically, it is my home. But Somalia feels like home in a way I'm not sure how to explain. It's like that nostalgic feeling you get when you meet someone who feels like you grew up with them. Someone you've never met but who somehow feels familiar. Somalia is like that. A friend you never met, but you feel like you know.

~

My friends are my support system. My friends are extraordinarily supportive, especially one in particular. We relate to each other based on our relationships with our families. We talk about those struggles, and it's a sensitive subject. But my friends are super understanding and comforting. They're amazing, sweet, good people. They're always there for me. It's nice to have a shoulder to lean on. We walk each other through any issues we're having. And we unconditionally support each other.

My education at dugsi left me wanting for something more. I felt a huge sense of frustration. Every weekend, I would focus solely on memorizing passages from the Qur'an. But I wasn't being taught the meaning of the text I was reciting. The beauty of the Qur'an wasn't touching my heart. It made me think, *Who am I doing this for?* I wasn't necessarily doing it for myself. And I wasn't doing it for the sake of Allah (سبحانه وتعالى). I was doing it because it made my parents happy. That made me feel guilty because my intentions were corrupted in this way. It felt like a performance instead of a genuine act of worship. We were learning the Qur'an, but we weren't living by it. I hated feeling like a hypocrite. I'm glad my parents took me to a low-key, out-of-the-way dugsi program, because there was a big, well-known dugsi I could have attended. I'm glad I didn't, because in hindsight, I'd heard a lot of interesting tales. I feel like dugsi warped my relationship with Islam. Because the teachings were superficial, my relationship to Islam was undeveloped. I was on autopilot for my diin. Which is okay to an extent, while you're figuring things out and making meaning for yourself, but I was not being taught to see that beauty. It was more a focus on punishment and consequences. If we do something, it's "just because," not because there is a story or meaning attached to it. How can you form a connection to something like that? I never doubted my faith, but I doubted the way I was being taught. We have a merciful Creator, and all we're learning is hell and punishment? That didn't sit well with me. That's why I feel bad for people who leave the faith. I always think, *What was their experience?* They probably weren't shown the depth of Islam, and of course that would weigh on someone. The best example of Islam we can show the world is ourselves: Are we being kind to each other? How are we representing our faith?

One day my mom was talking to another mom, and she mentioned a woman who does dugsi and Islamic studies on Fridays. My mom asked me if I wanted to join, and I said sure. I had been in another Muslim girls program before, at an organization. I enjoyed my time there because we would meet up on Fridays and do activities and have fun. It was nice to have a place to socialize specifically for us, because it's so rare to find those spaces for Muslim girls. It's the first place I started really seeing the storytelling and history in Islamic studies. Before that, I would go to dugsi on Saturday and Sunday. Learn, recite, and memorize. Rinse and repeat. I know a lot of people I grew up with felt the same way. We were not being engaged or challenged in a meaningful way. Memorization is great, but that's only one part of a giant puzzle. It would be like going to school and being taught only how to read. Reading is fundamental, but we also need to write, do math, learn science, learn history, etc. Dugsis feel like factories at this point, and people question why the kids grow up and are not coming back. At school, we're constantly being tested. Five days a week, we do tests and quizzes, and dugsi becomes another test on the weekend. We learn how to pass and perform, but did we really benefit from our studies, or are we just studying for another test? Dugsi was stressing me out in the same way as school, and I was completely disengaged. When do we get a chance to fall in love with the diin? When do we find our paths?

That's when I started another girls program with a female teacher. I always thought my beliefs toward dugsi were a personal problem that I needed to overcome on my own. But this class changed my life. Sister Ramla opened up to us right away and told us her life story. She talked about how she wasn't always religious and how she came to find her own way. What she was saying was so authentic. She had experienced exactly what we were going through. She wasn't this far-removed, perfect saint who judged us for our shortcomings; she's a grown-up who had her own set of trials and tribulations and wanted to help us understand ours. She gave us hope. This feeling was foreign because in regular dugsi we didn't have hope. It's about forcing yourself to do it for your parents or some other reason. I felt like I was building the confidence to engage with Islam on an organic level. I started seeing familiar faces in class, and soon my peers became my friends.

We attended every Friday for three years straight. We became close friends. This is what dugsi was missing: this sense of community. Being comfortable and having a sense of trust and closeness with your classmates. We grew up together. I knew these girls had my back. Throughout my life, having attended predominantly White schools and just growing up in my home situation, I was always trying to find myself. I always felt like I was doing things for other people or putting on for someone's sake, but Sister Ramla's class helped me find myself. I discovered what real friendships look like, what it is to have fun, and how to have healthy relationships with people. Ramla was a role model to us, and she was an adult I could message whenever and I knew she'd be there for me. I wish everyone could have this experience. We battle a lot as young people, and it's easy to lose sight of everything, especially with the diin. But having this support group can change your life. I knew I wasn't alone in anything. Sister Ramla showed us the love of diin. She taught us and showed the mercy, kindness, and love of Allah (سبحانه وتعالى). She was never judgmental with us, just understanding. It's how parents should be, but if they're not, kids should have at least one adult in their lives like that.

I can't help but contrast how I felt in this class and how I felt at dugsi. It makes me think of during the Prophet Muhammad's ﷺ time, when the Qur'an was being sent down and people had to change: they responded to gentleness better than harshness or complete restriction. I think no one is sitting kids down and explaining the beauty or the wisdom behind a certain tradition. That's a mistake, because the history is rich, and we're being deprived, in a way. We deserve to know our faith fully. I'm so grateful to Ramla and the girls I met in her group. They changed my life and my relationship to Allah (سبحانه وتعالى), which is the most important relationship I have today.

I was brought up wearing hijab, and I'm really grateful, because it's one of the aspects of the diin that comes easy to me. I know some people struggle with it and that's their test, but for me, it's something I feel comfortable in. And because it's not something that I had to battle with or something I consciously decided to put on for the first time, it's very natural to me. My mom did want me to wear jilbaab, but that's not something I wanted to do. She was content with me wearing my hijab, though. My hijab has become a part of my skin. I would feel naked without it. Imagine going outside without pants. You'd instantly be aware of the sensation because you're so used to wearing pants every day. It's like that for me. It's a part of who I am now.

I love seeing people come into their own with faith. With a lot of things, like the neighborhood we grow up in or the language we speak, faith is something inherited, not a conscious decision. I love that we have the privilege of being born into Islam, but I would love for people to take the time to explore and understand our faith. From my own experience, I've found that it fosters gratitude for what we might take for granted. And it allows people to find their own path. I find that if you don't have that intentional relationship with Allah (سبحانه وتعالى), it's not hard to get lost and caught up in the minutiae of life. Your traditions and obligations feel complex and tiresome; you become overwhelmed. But when you have purpose and clarity, you are driven by something bigger than you.

For Somali people, religion feels competitive, like sports and school. People brag about how beautifully their kids recite Qur'an or how much they've memorized. These are amazing accomplishments, but bragging or being arrogant muddles the intention and purpose of faith. Are we excelling for the sake of Allah (سبحانه وتعالى) or so we can show off, like our faith is a flashy sports car or mansion? Humility is a cornerstone of Islam.

If more folks took that seriously, they would approach their faith as less of a competition with others and instead as a competition with yourself. We're meant to fight our egos, not feed them.

~

In a hundred years, I hope my kids are still Muslim. And good people. That they spread and share kindness. Just be good and have diin. Same for five hundred years from now. I hope they still have a planet to inherit, because of all the climate change. That's one thing that scares me about what Allah (سبحانه وتعالى) will ask us—about the earth, about animals, and how we've treated them. I don't want to leave a negative impact on the earth.

I want to tell Somali people to stop allowing what other people think to stop you from doing what you want to do. Do what you love and live your life how you want to live it.

To young Somali women, please take time to find yourself. Take time to figure out who you are, because that's the number-one thing that will get you far in life. Taking care of yourself can vary from person to person. It can be doing self-care, reading a book, disappearing for a week, or enjoying your own company. There's a value in learning to be comfortable in your own shoes and being okay by yourself, enjoying being alone. This can help you learn to love yourself and be present in your own life.

I would just tell Somali men to go learn to love themselves and understand themselves. If you do that, you will learn how to understand and protect Somali women. When we learn to love ourselves and understand one another, we stop the cycle of hate.

4

Fartun Mohamed, 20s, Virginia
pseudonym

My name is Fartun. I am the firstborn of ten. My mom remembers my birth vividly. It was her scariest one for several reasons. It was her first pregnancy and delivery, so she was terrified of the ordeal and its unknowns. She was also in America, far away from home and family, especially her mother. I don't think my mom imagined experiencing childbirth without her own mother. Out of all my siblings, I was the only child she delivered without my dad present. My dad had to go to work and wasn't there when I was born. My mom was in labor for over sixteen hours. I was finally born in the wee hours of the morning on a cold day in Virginia. My mom named me after a good friend of hers back home.

My parents came to America very young, both in their early twenties. They met in a refugee camp in Kenya and got married in less than a month. My dad was on his way to America. My mom wanted to get out of the camp and go to the West. Anywhere—it didn't matter, as long as she didn't spend the rest of her life in that camp. My mom's friend told her about her cousin who was leaving soon and that he could take a wife. She set them up to meet, and my parents agreed. My dad said to my mom that they didn't have to get married. But they actually liked each other and very soon wanted to get married. In Somali, we say, "Wax walba waa calaf," and that means everything is in fate. It was destined to happen.

When they came to the States, they were very confused at the airport. They were supposed to go to a home of a friend, but they didn't know how to navigate in a foreign country. They didn't speak English at all. An African American woman noticed their confusion and approached them. Somehow, they were able to understand each other enough for her to drive them to their destination. She kept saying something along the lines of "we're the same," as in Black and from Africa, and so we have to help each other. My parents never forgot this stranger's kindness.

We lived in Virginia for a short time before resettling in Minnesota. I hated school in Virginia. We went to a predominantly Black inner-city school. At that time, there weren't many Somalis or Muslims at this school. My mom dressed me in those matching skirt-blouse sets and hijab. I stuck out like a sore thumb. Anytime you are different as a kid, you're already a target. I was bullied by older and bigger kids, a mixture of boys and girls. They would call us African booty scratchers and taunt us relentlessly. My brothers had the luck of blending in with the other kids. They wore the same clothes, and you couldn't tell them apart from the other students. But I wore hijab and was visibly different, and kids don't take too kindly to different. I was mocked for my skin, features, clothes—anything they could come up with to bully me.

What drives me nuts is now as an adult living in a predominantly Black neighborhood, I see my siblings face the same anti-Blackness we went through. One time, my nine-year-old sister got off the bus after school. I used to sit on the stoop to greet my siblings and welcome them home each day. I saw a woman in a car honk and cuss out my sister for absolutely no reason as she crossed the street. This woman was shouting derogatory names at the top of her lungs and scared my sister. My sister was in a group of African American kids and Asian kids, and this woman singled her out because she's Somali. My blood was boiling, but the woman took off by the time I reached the street. What reason could she possibly have for being so vile to a child? How are you treating another person this way when you know what it's like to be discriminated against? When you know what it's like for somebody to be prejudiced against you because of something you have absolutely no control over? How do you treat a child with no humanity? My sister is a sweet little girl who tries to make friends with everyone. She's had kids say they couldn't be friends with her anymore because she's Somali. Kids don't understand at that age that people have their own problems and might internalize other people's prejudice. I tried to protect my siblings from that. It hurts me to see it.

My parents had heard that Minnesota was a land of opportunity. It had good schools and social services. But most of all, it had a large community of Somalis. Finally, a home away from home. We moved around a ton in Minnesota. We spent the first ten years in Minneapolis. After that, we moved around from metro cities to the suburbs. Even when we lived in the same home in Minneapolis for years, we were constantly changing schools. I went to a new school each year. I went to public schools, private schools, and charter schools. My mom was always searching for something better. Our household wasn't always stable, but she wanted us to go to the best schools and live in the best neighborhoods. Her guiding compass was her kids. I admire that in my mom.

But moving around a lot also caused issues for me. My biggest problem was keeping friends. I felt like I could never really get close to anyone, because the second I did, I would walk home to find moving boxes and a U-Haul truck. It made me a super quiet kid who mostly kept to myself. It was only when I got older that I became more outspoken.

In school I mostly felt invisible. Because I was a quiet kid, it was kinda easy for my teachers to forget about me. I don't blame them; I'm sure it's hard keeping track of thirty kids every day. I was constantly new to schools, and nobody had a connection to me. My teachers didn't know my siblings; they didn't know my friends or really anything about me. My philosophy was, why have people get to know me when I'm not gonna be here long anyway? I didn't have any roots. I always envied the kids who would say, "Oh, we've known each other since the first grade."

The few friends I made are now from all over the metro. We've formed lifelong bonds from our school days, and we get excited to run into each other as adults. It's our shared experience and memories that have glued us together.

I was ripped away from my favorite school right as I was entering middle school. My household got rearranged, and I had to go live with my grandmother and aunt. I then attended a school in Eagan, Minnesota. It was absolute torture. I had no friends. It was a mostly White school, and I rarely saw anyone who looked like me. The only windows were in the stairs, the only glimpse of the outside world we had. It was a real-life prison. I developed an eating disorder and dissociative issue. I felt like I would leave my body during school. I would tell myself, *It's gonna be 3:15. I'm gonna be home soon. I'm gonna make it.* I repeated that in my head every day. My grades were terrible. I never looked at my homework. I had no friends either. I had just one escape: books. I loved reading so much. Books were my safe place. I just felt like I could disappear into a book and be gone. I'm not here anymore. I'm not in Eagan. I'm not living with my grandma. I'm in this book. I'm living this character's life. At this school there was a librarian who was really nice to me. He was always recommending books to me. He even overlooked rules for me. He knew I wasn't supposed to spend all that time in the library, but he never snitched. If he saw me skipping class to read, he would gently nudge me to go to class. Sometimes I would get out in the middle of my class and just go to the library and read a book the whole time. He'd see me there, and he wouldn't say anything. That was the only joy I had during this miserable time.

~

Mom worked in factories when she was younger. She saved up for a store and eventually got one. She's the definition of a hustler. Always stacking paper and investing in land and properties. She came here with nothing and fought to build something for us to inherit. Early on in my parents' marriage, they had more traditional roles. My mom started working so she could send money back home to her family without having to worry about my dad having enough or disagreeing. She studied English, got her driver's license, and got a GED. She was able to sponsor a lot of her family. Fun fact: our family was on flight thirteen. Flight thirteen was a plane with Somali refugees that arrived in the United States. Somalis who came early to the States and assimilated quickly were called "flights" for that reason. The stereotype is that someone on an early flight is a FOB who thinks they're better than other Somalis because they assimilated to main-stream culture. The joke is that they did a poor job assimilating, and they are easily identified as an immigrant.

Over time, my parents' roles switched, and she became the main provider. It damaged their marriage. He depended on her to bring home money, and he became another mouth to feed. That completely changed their relationship. That's when my dad started chewing khat. He became bitter and resentful. It messed him up as a person. It really did. And it got to the point where people were always praising my mother for being such a hard-working woman. It was as if everything that he did for his wife and family was erased. It was gone. It ate away at him. Because he was in trouble with the law, my mom would threaten to call his parole officer during arguments. I thought that hit below the belt.

Through it all, I was my mom's confidante. I remember when I was six years old, my parents had a nasty fight and my dad stomped out to cool off. She woke me up from my bed and pulled me into the kitchen. She rehashed the whole fight and the things my dad had done. We would sit at the dinner table, and my mom would tell me everything and then ask, "What should I do?" And I had no idea. But I had to come up with something because she needed my help. I would tell her to talk to him and try to work it out. I didn't want to see my parents fight and I didn't know these things about my dad. She would talk to me like I was an adult when I was at a super young age. She would warn me about never trusting anyone and tell scary stories to drive the point home. My mom was a lonely woman. Even in her marriage, I know she felt like she was alone. Even though she had family and friends here, she felt alone. She turned to me for comfort. In a way, I never got to be a kid, not only in my responsibilities but in the way I was treated.

I was responsible for my siblings and got punished whenever they got in trouble. I had to keep my brothers in line, and if they did something wrong, I got in trouble because I was the oldest. I had such a confusing relationship with my mom. It messed me up psychologically because in one way, I was my mom's best friend and confidante. At the same time, she was the person who caused me the most pain and torment. Whether it was physical or verbal, my mom's abuse hurt the most. She was my mom. She loved me the most of anybody. I loved her too, to the point where I had an unhealthy attachment to her. I think a lot of it has to do with the fact that for my whole, entire life, she was working. I don't remember her not working. When I was sexually abused, she was away at work. I'm supposed to be the responsible one, the one who protects my siblings. But who was protecting me? I think being the eldest made me more compassionate toward my whole family. I want to do whatever I can to help them. I feel this extra sense of responsibility when it comes to me trying to help them out, or whatever. But I don't think they have the same for me. I don't think anyone does. I think everyone expects me to care for them.

I love my siblings so much. I remember bringing them home from the hospital and changing all their diapers. As their older sister, I tried to protect them from what I went through. I tried to give them a better chance at life. I feel a lot of guilt over them, because I don't think I've succeeded in that. I feel like I wasn't there for them enough during the times I was going through my own issues. I think gender had a lot to do with it. Because I was a girl, I was always responsible for my siblings. I had to make sure the house was clean and everyone's homework was done. But I couldn't play soccer outside with the boys. "Who do you think you are? A boy?" they would say. I used to imagine my life as a boy. Why wasn't I born a boy? If I was born a boy, none of these things would be happening to me, you know? I would have no responsibilities. Nobody could lay a hand on me. Would I have been sexually abused if I were a boy? Nothing happened to my brothers, and they were living in the same house with me. I felt like maybe I'd be loved more, I'd be protected more. I could have just lived my life, played soccer all I wanted. I would just be happy. All that good stuff. Maybe I would have gotten a chance to just be a kid, if I were a boy.

My dad worked construction early on. He eventually started working handyman jobs. He would go to different states working hard labor and send money home.

The thing I can say about my dad is he's always been a generous man. If he has it and someone asks, he'll give it away. Even if you're a stranger. We have a tumultuous relationship. I resent him for how he's treated my mother and how he didn't step up for my siblings and me. He's lashed out at me and my siblings physically and verbally. I tried to understand him, but my patience wore thin. My mom's side never liked my dad much. I think it was because deep down they always felt like my mom could do better. She was smart, beautiful, and ambitious. My grandfather begged her to go back to school, but she laughed it off. She had kids and a husband. This was it, she thought. I wish she had gone back and gotten an education. She might've been working a regular nine-to-five job instead of juggling work 24/7.

My mom is very religious. She grew up in Somalia in the eighties. And at this time in Somalia, people weren't very religious. People would still learn Qur'an, and Sufism was popular. But it was different. My mom was a teenager who really wanted to learn the diin. She was encouraged by other girls in the neighborhood. They taught her the importance of hijab. She brushed them off at first, but eventually she got closer to them and started learning from them. She wanted to cover up the way they did and searched her house for something to fashion together. She took a curtain and wrapped it around herself. She started going to dugsi.

Her brothers questioned her. They didn't like what she was doing. The family didn't like it because at that time religious people were seen as extremists. People were very much secular, and so to stand out wearing hijab was strange and looked down upon by some people. My grandmother was unhappy with her. Her brothers were accusing her of being intimate with macalamiin as an explanation for why she was practicing this way. She came home from dugsi and her older brother beat her up. My grandfather came home and beat his son to a pulp and told him to never put his hands on my mother again. My grandfather went to my mother. He asked her what was going on. He never had problems with her before, so the situation shocked him. My mom explained that she really wanted to practice Islam and learn the Qur'an. She said that she really wanted to wear her hijab and that this is what she decided for herself. He told her that nobody would stand in her way. Go ahead. My mom was a part of the protests to wear hijab in school. She was arrested and spent a day in jail fighting for her rights. Because of how hard she had to fight to practice Islam, she appreciates it that much more.

~

I got to experience going on Hajj when I was younger and stayed with my grandmother, whom I became very close to. She picked me to go with her because I was already probably her favorite. Before then, I had a religious awakening at a young age. I enjoyed praying and loved my Islamic studies classes. I asked my mom if I could wear those big hijabs. It was really obvious to my mom that I was a religious kid.

One of my most cherished memories of faith was making the pilgrimage to Mecca. Hajj changed my life. I have to admit, I did complain some, but only because I didn't know we're not supposed to! Insh'Allah I get a do-over as an adult. It was physically taxing. The scorching Arabian sun, the desert heat, and long walks were a lot to ask of a kid. We slept in tents and visited historic Islamic sites I had only read about in books or heard about from my teachers. Islam came to life during my trip. It was only seven days, but when it was all said and done, I came out different. Transformed. I didn't feel like the same, whiny preteen who went in. I felt purified.

I loved Hajj, but I hated being in Saudi Arabia. Our cultural differences were never more evident during my trip. After Hajj, we stayed with my cousin in his apartment. One day, I was standing on the balcony, just enjoying the cool evening. And all of a sudden, I heard violent and insistent honking. I looked down at the street to see this Arab guy cursing and yelling at me. He stepped out of his car and was shouting for me to go back inside, calling me names. I was freaked out by this random man yelling at me. Traffic came to a stop, and it felt like the entire city was looking at me. My cousin heard the commotion and came to the balcony to usher me inside. He told me that these people are strange and to always wear my hijab. I couldn't believe it. All this commotion because I wasn't wearing a hijab? This complete stranger spotted a twelve-year-old on the third-floor apartment balcony without a hijab and felt possessed to curse me out? I couldn't believe the cruelness of this place. I never stood on that balcony again. I couldn't wait to leave the country.

The next place we went to was Syria. It's the polar opposite of Saudi. The Syrians were the nicest people I had ever met. If the Saudis were cold and terrifying, the Syrians were warm and friendly. They welcomed us over and over again, smiling from ear to ear. They helped us with our bags and insisted on helping us get a taxi. The country was a marvel to witness. Mountain terrain and hills that never end. Grassy knolls and starry nights that take your breath away. The streets were paved with cobblestone, and the homes were packed close together. The front doors seemed perpetually open, homes bustling with people dashing in and out during all hours of the day. There was always something to explore. We went to museums and historic sites. We walked around the city at night, eating greasy and comforting Syrian food from vendors. The street food was magnificent and a beloved part of our outdoor excursions. We couldn't stop eating the delicious food. The city smelled of cream and coffee; how could a city smell so good? I would step out on my hotel balcony and see the mountains capped with snow in the distance. Peace and beauty. How could you not fall in love? It was as if Syria had been created simply to captivate all of the senses.

After having lived in the West, Middle East, and Africa, I can say I'd truly never seen anything like Syria. It was the first place I saw Christians, Muslims, and Jews living in harmony. Peace was an understatement. There was no animosity and violent bigotry. Everyone was nice to us. I couldn't get over their kindness and sincerity. It wasn't just Syrians; it was all the people who lived there. There was something about Syria that made people see each other as brothers and sisters, despite their obvious differences. I met one Syrian woman who opened up to me about her life in the country. She had six kids and was a second wife. She was so happy and full of life. She was easy to talk to, and I was very fond of her. Every time we'd go to the market or go out in the city, she would knock on a stranger's door and ask if she could come in to pray. It could be a Muslim, Jew, or Christian. And every time, they would let her in to pray. This wasn't just on her behalf; this was how kind the Syrian people are. They would have done it for anyone. I remember when I came back to the States, I told my mom that I was going to live in Syria when I grew up.

I remember the Arab Spring distinctly. Every day we'd hear from Twitter or the news about a bomb or air strikes. I became super obsessed with the news. For the first time ever, what was happening in another country was affecting me directly. This wasn't a random country, so far removed from me that I could afford to ignore it. It was personal. I knew those streets and neighborhoods. It's the place where students came to seek Islamic knowledge for centuries, and history was etched into the bones of the city. Ancient literature, artifacts, historic sites, libraries, and architecture. What Syria produced could never be replicated.

Most of all, I knew those people. They were good people who had been so kind and sweet to anyone who visited them, and now their home was destroyed. It was so heartbreaking. Syria was the place I wanted to spend the rest of my life. To see Syrian refugees being denied asylum all over the world was even worse. How cruel. I kept thinking, *Syrians wouldn't do that to you.* I remember seeing Somali refugees in Syria, and they were living happily ever after. Syrians welcomed whoever needed help into their country. I think if you never leave America, you have a hard time imagining the rest of the world and all its inhabitants. You might think this is the best country in the world and that other people are not quite like you. When you hear about a school being hit by a drone strike or a casualty number on the news, you might see those deaths as mere numbers on a screen. But if only you knew how thin the difference is that separates your comfortable life from others', you would empathize more often. You would see their humanity. Especially when they've lost their homes.

In high school, I went to Xamar for a year. My mom wanted my siblings and me to learn Qur'an and remember the culture. It's not that we had forgotten, but my mom insisted that we never forget our faith and traditions. That's what led me to Somalia to stay with my dad's family for a year. My siblings were already there, and when I came, I assumed the position of mom. I was judged by my extended family for having returned. Back home, there's a perception that if you get sent for dhaqan celis, it's because you're a bad kid who needs to be reformed. That wasn't the case for me, but the judgment loomed over my head. I would constantly be viewed with suspicion and accused of things I wasn't doing. I met a lot of family. I met my paternal grandmother, who is not my favorite person. She was needlessly cruel and judgmental. I had to defend myself against her when she would lash out unprovoked. We also fought because I would tattle to my mom about the goings-on of the home.

At the time, we were staying with my grandmother. Back home, a person could host many different families at once. Soon my aunt and her kids moved in. We didn't get along. My dad's side did not like my mom and were disrespectful. I couldn't tolerate disrespect, especially of my mom. I would be in a lot of fights. More people would come in and out. You were at the mercy of whoever's house it is. I didn't have many friends except for the maids my grandma hired. They were genuine, kind, and close to me in age. I felt like everyone else had a guard up against them because of their station in life. But I formed close relationships with them while we cleaned the home or prepared dinner together.

But it wasn't just the maids who were looked down on; it was anyone who didn't have someone who could protect them. For example, my grandmother's nephew had a daughter. When the nephew died, his daughter came to live with my grandmother. Her mom didn't want her and would call her all sorts of horrible names. Her mother even called her bad luck on account of her dad's death. She was so abused and hated. That's why my grandma took her in. When my other aunt came, she was so cruel to this girl. In Islam, you're supposed to treat orphans with respect. My aunt treated her like Cinderella, forced her to slave away and do degrading things like wash her soiled menstrual underwear. I was completely repulsed. Although my grandmother wasn't cruel to this girl, she wouldn't intervene to stop her daughter's abuse. I just didn't understand it. This woman would pick on anyone who couldn't defend themselves from her. And she would get away with it! I would get in trouble for speaking out.

One day, my aunt was being exceptionally cruel to our maid. She was a seventeen-year-old girl, and she told me how she was out here by herself trying to save money to send back home to her parents. My aunt made the girl upset about some chore done wrong, and she ran outside to the courtyard to cry by herself. I went out to comfort her, and my aunt followed, continuing to yell at the girl and call her useless and dramatic. I finally had enough and told my aunt to leave the girl alone. My aunt turned her attention to me and mocked me for being friends with maids, as if it were an insult to be friends with someone of a lower station. I had had enough and cursed her out in Somali for the first time. My grandma came outside and slapped me for disrespecting her daughter. She kept slapping me, and I was done with this family.

I called my mom. I already wasn't feeling well physically. Everyone in the house started giving me the cold shoulder. I felt really sick. I told my mom I was sick and cried uncontrollably. She sent her cousin from the city to come and get me to the hospital. This was disrespectful to my grandma because I was in her care, but my mom didn't care. At the hospital, I found out I had malaria and typhoid at the same time. My mom cut me a ticket, and I was back in America.

I traveled to the continent a couple more times as I got older. I met my grandfather. He's the patriarch of our tribe. He had a lot of love for me, and I felt it. I was very close to him. Each time I visited, it became so apparent to me how much my family relies on remittances. We all grow up with our parents sending money through the xawaalad, but unless you know the recipients, the transaction feels far removed from your life. But when you see up close how much one girl's tuition costs and what it means to her or what an uncle's medicine costs, it's hard to not personalize it. I became so grateful for the opportunities and resources I took for granted in the States. I developed a personal stake in the well-being of my relatives back home, who now had faces, names, and stories.

I fell in love with the continent each time I traveled. Whether

I was in Nairobi, Jigjiga, or Hargeisa, I gathered memories that would last me till the next time I visited. The air was clean, and the night sky twinkled so brightly I felt I could touch the stars. The food was unlike anything back home. The meat was fresh because animals were slaughtered fresh for the market. The fruits and vegetables were ripe and juicy. I couldn't stand American bananas upon my returns because I had just spent months eating the real thing. Whenever my grandma would complain about how life in America was nothing compared to back home, my siblings who had never left probably thought she was just complaining the way old folks do. But I knew exactly what she was talking about. The air, food, weather, scenery, and people just didn't compare. I was loathe to leave and couldn't wait to get back on a plane.

The last time I left for Africa was because my life was in a weird place. I was dealing with a lot at home and wasn't sure what my next move would be. I felt impatient, depressed, and uncertain. I wanted to find clarity in my purpose. I was longing to find my life. I was twenty-one, and I wanted to start my family. People just expect you to get married around that time. I know my parents would've supported me, so I thought, *why not?* I had a bunch of adventures and my fair share of trials too. I fell in and out of love. When I came back, I was disappointed. I didn't get what I was looking for. I didn't have a crazy epiphany when I was in Africa. I thought I'd come back like Dave Chappelle—with answers and a sense of clarity. But I came back unresolved. In fact, I wanted to leave for Africa as soon as I set foot in the States. I didn't get a chance to deal with my issues of depression and anxiety. I didn't start my family. I didn't have anything to show for it. I was back in the same spot I had started.

One thing I kept experiencing on my travels was colorism. People could not stop talking about my skin color. They would ask me why I'm dark-skinned. I defied their image of what an American girl was supposed to look like. My whole family is dark-skinned; it's not something that's odd or unique to us; it's just how we are. It added to my self-consciousness as a teenager.

❧

When I came back from my first trip to Xamar, I was behind in school and had a lot of catching up to do. Schoolwork had piled up, and I was tossed back into my old responsibilities. Growing up, I didn't have much time to be a kid. I was changing diapers and bathing babies as early as four or five years old. I remember each of my sibling's births and being handed a kid to care for like a doll that had come to life. I went from playing with baby dolls to burping real babies. I wasn't considered one of the kids; I was one of the adults. I was essentially a third parent to my siblings.

My parents really wanted me to go to college. That's what they expected of me. I wasn't at all prepared for it. I was short on credits during high school. I didn't know how to apply or where to start. I asked one of my relatives for help, and she helped me figure out the application process. I was overwhelmed with FAFSA, GPAs, credits, and placement tests. I wish there was a smoother transition into higher learning. I enrolled in a community college. I didn't know what classes to take. I signed up for a 7:00 AM writing class. I didn't realize I could've picked a different time. My first semester was a whirlwind. Everything was a learning curve.

When I was in college, my mom was diagnosed with ovarian cancer. She was the primary provider for the family, with my dad intermittently picking up work. She would need to cut back and eventually stop working. My youngest siblings were energetic toddlers who needed constant supervision. The rest of my siblings were fairly young. My full-time studies required most of my day to complete. I had only just gotten into school and was exploring a possible career. Hearing my mom's diagnosis shook me to my core. I was faced with the mortality of the person I loved most in the world. The younger siblings looked to me to make it better, but there was nothing I could do. I was terrified. I couldn't imagine losing my mother. At first, everyone stepped up and helped out. Someone would drop off the kids while someone else got groceries. One by one, everyone fell off and things started falling apart. I would miss a day of class to look after the kids, and then those days started piling up. Sometime in the semester, I dropped out of all my classes without warning.

I didn't notify my professors or the school; I simply stopped attending.

I went into full-time care mode. I woke my siblings for breakfast and got them on the school bus on time. I cleaned the house, cooked meals, and did laundry in between prayers. My grandmother, who was living with us at the time, also required full-time care. I stepped up as her caretaker. I fed and bathed her, gave her medication on time, and took her to appointments and braided her hair. I listened to her stories and the duas she constantly made for our family. Most of all, I worried about my mother without pause. I went with her to appointments, I pestered her about eating the right food, and when she tried to take a shift to make ends meet, I insisted she rest so she could get better. I couldn't control much, but I refused to allow what fell within my control to go neglected. I was exhausted. My mom put on a brave front for me, but I knew she was scared. I was broken. She reminded me that nothing happened without the permission of Allah (سبحانه وتعالى). I prayed fervently for my mother. I monitored my mother's health like my own life depended on it. After time and treatment, my mother went into recovery. We celebrated her health. But quietly, I always feared what would happen if her cancer came out of remission.

I started experimenting with drugs during my mom's cancer. I used it to numb the pain. When I was a kid, I was super attached to my mom. I had a phobia of her leaving me. She worked a lot in order to take care of us financially. Even when I was an infant, she would leave me with my Korean babysitter in order to work. When I found out she might die, it was as if my worst nightmare was coming true. Before then, my mom and I were starting to have problems. I was hanging out with friends and staying out late. Kicking it at hookah lounges and experimenting with weed. I remember it was such an exciting time. There was this one place where all the Somalis would hang. Girls would dress up to the nines; it was a place to be seen. So my mom and I were butting heads. My parents weren't in a good place before the cancer. They would argue and argue. It hit my dad hard. The way he deals with pain is with khat. So he just chewed and chewed. But they got closer through the ordeal. Everyone did. You can't help but be humbled by death.

Alhamdulilah. I can't help but say Alhamdulilah every time I think about that period of my life. I've noticed that it's somehow become unfashionable for some to say Alhamdulilah after witnessing others' strife. But they miss the point. I remember there was a period in my life where I was having panic attacks and anxiety every day. I would be totally fine, but it would creep up on me right before I fell asleep. Suddenly, I was wrapped up in death, fear, and loneliness. I would break out in a cold sweat, heart pounding, gasping for air. And then as soon as I felt it, I began thinking to myself, *There are people who are dealing with something ten billion times worse than I am. And right now, my mind is playing games with me. I am freaking out about inevitable, uncontrollable forces, as if the more time I spend worrying, the closer I come to controlling them. No. You know what is real? My friends Omar and Abdirahman are dead. My friend's family just lost their little brother. That's permanent. That's tangible pain. Me? I'm home. I'm safe. I have my parents. I have everything. I'm good. If I'm not good now, I will be good soon. Alhamdulilah.* And then, *whoosh*, the anxiety leaves my body. That calms me down. It's not as though you're supposed to revel in the loss or suffering of others, but instead it should bring you back down to earth and remind you of what you have to be grateful for. It's not to look down on people. It's to recognize that they are being tested. And that you might be tested one day too, in that way.

Even though life in our home was bustling, the world outside had gone on without me. My friends were now graduating university, posing for pictures with their black gowns and decorated caps. I felt insecure and little. Who was I now? The dropout? The girl with nothing to show for herself? I maintained few friends, and I lost touch with most when I dropped out. I dreaded running into old friends in public. "How've you been? What are you up to?" was bound to come up. What would I tell them? "Oh, me? I dropped out to take care of my family and don't know what to do now. Lovely. And you?" I was embarrassed to have been left behind. I couldn't help but compare myself to my friends with degrees or kids or careers. Look how far they had come. But where was I? Drifting through my life, trying to make sense of what I knew and who I wanted to be.

My mom wasn't happy when I dropped out of school. She was upset with me. She was angry with me for disrupting my future. I couldn't believe it. Had she not seen how I stepped up to run the household and take care of the kids? I had to defend myself. That's when it dawned on me that I had to start thinking about myself. I still don't have the hang of it, but it's something I'm conscious of. I feel like my whole life I've been trained to put everyone else before me. It's almost a reflex. Something you don't have to think about, like breathing or the beat of your heart. But I realize that if I don't, no one else will. There will always be problems bigger than mine, needs more urgent than mine. I'm a natural nurturer, but that doesn't mean I should get left behind.

Currently I work at a company that makes medical devices. I want to go back to school for engineering. I've been in this industry for a while now, and it's really fascinating. I would love to be the person on the other side, designing and engineering these products.

~

I remember 9/11. I was home microwaving popcorn when everyone started freaking out. My uncles shouted for the TV to be turned on. I was used to watching Al Jazeera with my family and seeing bombings and violence in places like Palestine on the news. I couldn't believe this was America on the screen. Everyone was calling people to see if they had seen it. I went to the living room and looked up at the sky, waiting for us to get attacked next. Soon we heard the Pentagon was targeted. It felt like the world was ending. When I went back to school, the teacher was explaining what had happened and the whole class was looking back at me. I got mad. Wasn't I as scared as you all were? Why are you looking at me for answers? That's when it hit me. Oh. They thought it was my fault because I am a Muslim. I just kind of accepted it. I was not gonna fight with anybody. I'm not gonna get into verbal arguments because then they could very well arrest me and send me to Guantanamo Bay.

When I got older, I kept learning more and more. In college, we would debate about patriotism in our poli-sci classes. People say this thing: if you don't like it here, then leave. What kind of response is that to a reasonable debate about the role of government and policy? Is there a baseline political or partisan view that all Americans automatically hold—or is this a democracy? Am I supposed to be okay with the fact that George W. Bush just started a war in a country for no reason? People all thought this was normal because they were afraid and the facts didn't matter. People were willing to forfeit all their rights, just in case. Not to mention those who profited off of the war. When I saw the news about the war in Iraq or Afghanistan, it was gut-wrenching. I saw how little they would report on civilian casualties. Did no one care? It just showed me how selfish other Americans could be, that they thought a totally offensive war with a country that did nothing to us was somehow keeping us safe. All people needed was a story to be sold, on both sides, about either keeping our freedom or bringing it to others. Whatever you needed to hear to justify senseless war.

I've noticed some cultural differences in our generations. My mom's way of dealing with racism is to ignore it. Don't say anything, avert your eyes, and just walk away. I think it comes from fear. This idea that we're not gonna be respected by authorities if they intervene—or worse, our citizenship will get stripped. My mother's generation is afraid that a traffic ticket will be held against them. But their kids are bolder. Young people do not put up with it. We were born here. This is my land as much as it is yours, and to be honest, that's probably not saying much because of the diabolical way this land was obtained. There is really nothing you can do to me because I'm just as much of an American as you. You want me to go back to my country? You first.

I think what makes some people so angry about Somalis is the way we proudly carry ourselves. We still wear hijab and will excuse ourselves from work to pray. I speak my language perfectly, and I will speak it while I am waiting in a grocery line. And what about it? We don't cower and hide ourselves. We instead say, "If I was meant to die, it's fate." We got here by the will of God. There are refugees trying to seek asylum in this country today who are being denied. That could've easily been us. But God put sympathy in people's hearts, and that's why we're here. Another boat carrying refugees capsized the other day, and the US Navy watched and did nothing. They lack empathy for human life. It's here today, gone tomorrow. At the end of the day, I have to thank God for putting empathy in people's hearts and making a way.

At the same time, we are losing parts of our culture in the migration. Things are different. Kids are raising their voices at their moms and talking crazy. People don't respect elders the way they used to. Even if your elder is wrong, walk away; there's no reason to be in a shouting match with an old person. That sounds crazy even to imagine. What I hope for myself and others is that we take the best parts of both cultures and be better people. My fear is that we instead choose the worst of both and become monsters. I like our values of kinship and hospitality in Somali culture. I like how highly we respect education as well. In American culture, I appreciate moderation and individualism, when it's not taken to an extreme. The ability to make your own way and choose a life for yourself as an accepted norm is delightful. As Somali Americans, we can observe the best of both cultures and inspire each other to new heights.

There are programs that target and violate the rights of Muslim Americans in this country. If anything, I feel like that kind of behavior made my faith stronger because first of all it's just so messed up that we're being targeted to begin with. At the end of the day, I want to know that I still have the choice to practice my faith and not be persecuted for doing so. It's also made people more cautious, because even mundane comments can be viewed under a hypercritical lens by virtue of the speaker being Muslim. We're limiting our speech because of the fear and paranoia of others. Our participation in activism and politics is viewed as suspicious. So which is it: should we assimilate and be civically engaged in our democracy, or can we do that only when we agree with our critics' exact politics?

My relationship with hijab has been a roller coaster. I don't wear hijab right now. I wore jilbaab when I was younger, around the age of eight or nine. I really wanted to wear it. But somewhere along the way I left it behind. I hope one day I can improve my relationship with it because I respect the purpose of the hijab. Sometimes I feel hopeless. And sometimes I feel like maybe there is hope. I just want to be on the path of the believer, the righteous, pious Muslim. I want to be that.

~

I'm Black. You see that the first time you look at me. Ethnically I'm Somali, but I feel like in our culture we always have such a hard time differentiating the two. People identify in different ways. When I was a kid, I had a hard time reconciling the two. We kind of always knew that we weren't accepted by the African American community and that we were different, not quite American. So in that sense I knew I was Somali first. I think other people conflate race and ethnicity. I think a lot of it has to do with our faith. We are visibly Muslim, and sometimes that's hard to understand within the image we have of what it means to be Black in America. We're all those things: Black, Muslim, Somali, African, American, immigrants, and so on. We've got anti-Blackness and prejudice that we need to confront in our community too. I think it's gonna take honest conversations in our communities in order for us to address anti-Blackness, colorism, and prejudice. That requires taking a deep look at our own assumptions and biases and seeing the humanity in one another.

When I was a kid, I was super proud of being an American. I was born and raised here. I was vibing with everyone, and their race didn't matter to me. If we vibe, we vibe. I remember reciting the Pledge of Allegiance every morning. Then you get older and you start to learn the dark truths about this country. My first best friend was a girl named Nicki. She was half White and half Native American. She identified as Ojibwe. She told me about Pilgrims and what White people did to Native Americans. She told me how horrible Thanksgiving was. She taught me about her traditional dress and showed me a dance. I didn't know there were so many tribes and languages. She taught me about beautiful things in her culture. And she also taught me about an American history that was different from the one we were learning in class.

In school we learned very basic information about slavery and civil rights. It was only when I began my own research that I discovered how much had been left out. I learned about the Reconstruction era, Black Wall Street and the Tulsa Race Massacre, Jim Crow, mass incarceration, redlining, and so many other damaging policies and periods in American history. It was the first time what I was learning in school had been challenged. It wasn't the fairy tale of American exceptionalism we were told. In college, I learned about internment of Japanese Americans and other glossed-over histories. It made me always look for the other side, to seek the quiet truths.

⁓

In my efforts to battle with my demons, I fell into substance use and addiction. I needed help. Our community has different ways of dealing with shame. When you're a boy and you want to leave the lifestyle and change, you are welcomed back with open arms. Your past is seen as a folly of youth, an almost inevitable circumstance of being young. But when you're a girl, it's much harder. You're seen as damaged goods. You're seen as dishonorable and irredeemable. I don't think it's easy to grasp the full weight of being irredeemable. In Islam, we're taught that no action or sin is so great that you cannot repent to our Creator. That as long as we are human, we fall short, but what counts is that we try to embody the principles and values of Islam. But in our culture, we view some sins as beyond God's mercy and forgiveness.

What does it mean to be beyond forgiveness? What does it mean when some would rather you be dead than taint the name of your family? It feels like carrying the weight of the ocean and being punished when you falter and spill a single drop. It's hard to seek rehabilitation because to do so means admitting you have a problem. And admitting you have a problem means you have failed yourself and your family. What happens when your addiction is both a medical issue and a moral one? How do you rehabilitate a problem you're not supposed to have? I went through years of self-loathing and self-destructive behaviors. My world fell apart. I was able to self-rehab through the mercy of Allah (سبحانه وتعالى). I cut off a lot of people and took it one step at a time. I tried to find faith-based institutions that could help, but they were all geared toward Christianity. I came up with my own strategies based on trials and errors. It's still something I'm working through and very mindful of. Ultimately, I wish we had better ways of helping people through addiction, especially girls.

Through it all, my faith has been my rock. Islam helped me take care of myself. When I had no one to turn to, I turned to Allah (سبحانه وتعالى). It gave me something to believe in that was bigger than myself. It connected me to something that was permanent and unshifting. I found the courage to forgive myself and the people who had harmed me. Just like it was for my mother, Islam means so much to me now because I know what it's like to be without faith. I had to fight to believe in and practice it. Through fighting for it, I fought for myself. I don't put anything above my peace of mind and wellness now. I've learned the value of it above all else.

~

To Somali Americans, we're so special. We're the first of our kind. I feel like we should be happy for the experiences we've had. It wasn't the best. It wasn't rainbows and butterflies and flowers. I've dealt with a lot of depression. And a lot of it was me always asking why I was put on this earth. I feel like I've just gotten to the point where I stopped asking that question, Alhamdulilah. We all have a purpose. We're special. Our experiences made us who we are. The good things, the horrible things, and everything in that gray space. We're here for a reason. I think about our ancestors before us. We don't know all that they faced being controlled by another people in their own country. Being told they can't speak their own language, being stripped of their rights. They went through a lot of hardships. We too will endure hardships. But with every hardship comes ease. Find the little things that make it worth it.

To Somali girls, please know that you cannot be erased. I feel like in our culture we have this tendency to make Somali girls feel like they are so small and insignificant. But at the end of the day, you realize that through our mothers and our grandmothers, women are literally the ones who are holding this culture up. We're the ones who have held fast to our traditions. We're the ones who wear hijab despite the adversities that can come with it. And whatever hardship we go through, we will overcome it because we're so strong. Listen to the stories of your mother and her mother before her and her mother and so forth. You will be blown away by their wisdom. Shout-out to Somali girls everywhere. When you look to Somali women, you see greatness. We see the greatness you are achieving and the greatness you are capable of.

To Somali men, be supportive, be appreciative. Be thankful that you have Somali women. That the women who are your mothers, your sisters, your aunties, your cousins have given you so much. Thank God that you have a Somali woman in your life. That you have a mother who's Somali. That you have a sister who's Somali. That you have a cousin who is Somali. Be thankful that Allah (سبحانه وتعالى) made Somali women your counterparts. Protect them, help them flourish, don't dim their light. Don't limit your women; uplift them. Don't be an anchor that holds them down: be the wind that carries them higher.

5

Anisa Ali, 20s, Mogadishu, Somalia

I was born in Mogadishu. I was my parents' first child. My mom was a first-time mother and didn't know what to expect with her pregnancy. She remembers not even being sure of when to eat because of the fullness of her belly. She was lucky to be near family, but the process was difficult nonetheless. Our neighborhood was not safe. This was during the aftermath of the Civil War, but we were still in a period of danger and uncertainty. My dad finally had had enough when it became difficult to walk to the marketplace. Back home, most people go to the market every day and make meals fresh. If you can't get to the market, you might not be able to meet your basic needs.

We left for Addis Ababa, Ethiopia. My mom, three siblings, and I lived in the neighboring country while my dad went to the States. He saved up enough money to sponsor us years later. My time in Addis Ababa was filled with days at dugsi. My siblings and I went to dugsi every day. That's what I remember most about my life then.

I was raised in a traditional Somali household. My dad was the provider; he worked as a taxi driver. Mom was responsible for the household and our day-to-day needs. She also worked in home care and worked with disabled clients. Their jobs were impacted by the pandemic, and they lost work.

Being the eldest comes with a lot of expectations and responsibilities. It means growing up fast. I was always aware that I had to be a good example to my siblings. My parents emphasized my significance as their role model. I was also the de facto third parent. I was the translator, appointment booker, and accompanier to my siblings' parent-teacher conferences. No, they weren't my kids, but they basically were. Since the next closest sibling is five years younger than me, I see my siblings as little kids. At this point in life, we can't relate to too much of each other's experiences. We don't have the same expectations, and I always feel responsible for my siblings. I love them dearly.

The Somali Civil War is not something I talk to my parents about or something they sat me down to discuss. I've heard stories in passing over the years. My mom said she remembers constant fear, especially at night. No one was allowed to leave the home after maghrib because that's when the war was really fought. She remembers helicopters spraying people with pepper spray, people protesting, and not being allowed to join the protests. If it was safe, I know we would've stayed. Nobody really wants to leave home unless they have to.

~

When we arrived in the States, we moved to Minneapolis. I went to a charter school in St. Paul. I struggled every day because I knew absolutely nothing. No math, science, or English. My classmates, who were also new to the country, had at least attended formal school before immigrating and knew most everything except the English language. Before we left Ethiopia, my mom tried to enroll me in a regular school in order to acclimate me to school in America. It didn't work out, but I did gather basic conversational English. It didn't do me much good, because most Americans don't speak in formal English speech. Here I was prepared to say, "Hello, how are you?" and someone would respond, "Hey, what's up?" and my world would be turned upside down. No one prepared me for colloquial English, a language of its own.

While my classmates learned about rock formations, the Louisiana Purchase, and polynomials, I was learning all that and the culture, language, and norms of a new country. My first two years felt like an American immersion program.

After a while, my parents moved us to a small town about two hours south of the Twin Cities. Like many immigrant parents, they were on the search for something better for their family. Winona, Minnesota, is a small and predominantly White town east of Rochester, Minnesota. I started my freshman year of high school at Winona. There were maybe fewer than ten other non-White students—Asian, Black, and Hispanic—at my school. I wore full hijab or jilbaab and abayad and stuck out like a sore thumb.

I experienced an unparalleled amount of bullying right from the jump. I lined up for the school bus near my home where a bunch of kids were already waiting. As soon as I approached, the students began snickering and whispering to one another. I ignored them and patiently waited. The bus pulled up and everyone began filing in. I was the last person, and as I climbed the bus steps, the bus driver gawked at me in confusion. It was like an alien had appeared before him and he couldn't believe his eyes. He asked me who I was, and I told him I was a new student and that it was my first day. He refused to believe me, and I had to show ID to get onto the bus. The kids stared me down as I made my way to the back of the bus. I was not off to a great start.

My classmates were not sure what to make of me. They hadn't seen anyone like me in person before. One student asked me if I was an exchange student, imagining I had just arrived from some far-off, distant land. I misunderstood and replied "Yes." His eyes lit up, and he asked me where I was from. "Uhh . . ." I awkwardly began, "Minneapolis." He looked at me in confusion but left it alone. It wasn't until years later I realized what an exchange student is and why "Minneapolis" was probably not the answer he was expecting.

The teachers and staff didn't know what to do with me. I was an anomaly. I asked my homeroom teacher for a place to pray. I think I startled her with my request. I had stumped her. She took me to the counselor's office while they brainstormed a place for me to pray. Aha! They proudly took me to a small room that was adjacent to the band room. Unfortunately, the music was too loud for me to be able to pray in that room. So they took me to another room. That room happened to be on the other side of the school and would ultimately make me late to my class if I had to make the trek every day. Eventually, they found an office upstairs that I could use. I didn't realize there was a speaker attached to the intercom system in the room. At our school, they played music over the intercom between classes. Because the teacher and counselor had made such an effort already, I decided to not bother them again. I recited my Qur'an extra loud so I could hear myself during salat. I laugh at how it must've looked. In hindsight, I wish I had spoken up to see if there was a way to turn off the speakers in the room or find another place to pray. I didn't really see it as an option then.

The most interesting part of my experience might have been observing and negotiating cultural differences. For example, I had one teacher who always tried to make eye contact with me during conversations. She found it rude that I would avert my gaze when we'd talk and thought I was ignoring her or being disrespectful. It was quite the opposite. In our culture, we avoid direct gaze as a show of respect, especially to elders or respected people like teachers.

In other classes, students were expected to raise their hands and project their voice when called upon to answer a question or when they volunteered. I was uncomfortable raising my voice so loudly; it felt aggressive and rude. Besides, yelling felt so unnatural. So even though I knew the answers and was paying attention, I never raised my hand to share. My teachers would dock me points for participation and bring this up during parent-teacher conferences.

I was also self-conscious about handshaking. In Islam, we don't shake hands or touch people of the opposite sex. Even still, there is always a fear that a non-Muslim would interpret our broad rule on touch as a personal slight or rudeness. My first encounter with this was my middle school graduation. Our proud and eager male principal enthusiastically extended his hand after handing us our diplomas. I conceded and shook his hand because I didn't want him to think I was rude. For me, there's usually a slight apprehension about job interviews or meeting new people because I don't want someone meeting me for the first time to think I'm being impolite by not shaking hands. Shaking hands is really important in American culture, but there are other ways to greet one another, such as a smile or a hand over your heart.

I imagine most Muslims who are the first or new to a place

are like ambassadors of Islam. Whether we like it or not, how we engage, behave, and act will impact future Muslims in those roles or institutions. For example, I once worked at a major home improvement retailer. I asked my manager for time to go pray my daily salat. She said, "Well, the other Somali girls don't pray, so . . ." I told her that whether they pray or not has nothing to do with my prayer. If one person chooses not to pray, that doesn't inform how I practice my religion. She quickly said that's not what she meant; she was saying that the other girls don't ask for time to pray; they just pray whenever. I said again, that's on them, but when it reaches the time for prayer, I need to pray. She said why don't you pray whenever you're scheduled for breaks. I told her because that's not the time to pray. I can't just round up and accrue prayers like SkyMiles. Muslims pray their salat when it is the time to pray. She eventually allowed me to pray.

The only place I could find to pray was in the employee break room, a room that is usually loud and where people eat their lunch. I asked them for the longest time to provide another place for me to pray, and they would always say, "Yeah, for sure, we'll get you next time." But they never did. Even though I had to deal with skepticism and feet-dragging in order to pray at work, it was important for me to help build expectations for my supervisors so the next Muslim who worked there didn't have to go through an uphill battle to observe their religion. It's like when a company has a uniform policy for women to wear pants or not wear hijab. If there is a reasonable accommodation that can be made, I think it's important to pursue that so that there are more doors open for people. It's hard being the first, but someone has to.

During my sophomore year, my parents moved us back to Minneapolis. I enrolled at a local high school. My classmates were majority Black. Most teachers were White with a few Black, Asian, and Hispanic teachers. When I was leaving Winona High School, the school said I no longer needed to be placed as an English Language Learner, ELL. I was happy to leave ELL because I didn't like it being on my transcript. There is a stigma with ELL that you must be dumb or just not as smart as your peers. Unfortunately, my new school would not allow me to leave ELL because they had a different credits/grading system than my old school. My parents initially were supportive of my choice to leave, but after meeting with the school, they agreed that it would be best to remain in ELL. I was disappointed, but there was nothing I could do.

My ELL teacher was an Asian American with two dogs she loved very much. My first perception of her was as a nice, caring person. She was bubbly, hugged her students, and invited them to have lunch with her in her classroom. I would soon discover that she was the most racist person I had ever met. If my old teachers could be described as well intentioned and unaware, this teacher was manipulative and cruel.

Not only was she unkind, but she was also terrible at her job. It was an open secret that we did not learn anything in her class. Our teacher would go on and on about her pets, stopping every once in a while, only to launch back into uninteresting stories about her dogs. When she wasn't talking about her dogs, she would talk incessantly about herself. She would also teach her eleventh-grade students from children's picture books. At this school, ELL students also took regular English classes. Imagine writing an essay on Socrates in one class and then reading along to *If You Give a Mouse a Cookie* in another class. It was jarring and embarrassing, not to mention a waste of time.

As if being an ineffective teacher wasn't bad enough, she was also plain offensive. One day, we were going around the room answering a prompt about where we will go after graduation. When it was my turn, she stopped me before I could respond and said, "All Somali kids go to community college. Let me guess, a two-year college?" I was so mad; I couldn't even tell her off or respond to the original question. On another day, she told us, "I see a lot of students who will be back here next year," implying we would flunk and have to retake her class. "That's how I make my money!" she said with a laugh.

On top of that, she rarely graded our papers. Her grading system was as arbitrary as it was insane. She would dock me five or ten points for a missed comma or period, dropping my grade significantly for minor grammatical mistakes. I tried to tell my counselor about this teacher, but he brushed me off by telling me to make an appointment with her and work out our differences. I tried to meet with her for three months, but she kept dodging me. I confronted her one day and asked her if she would meet with me or not. She accused me of threatening her and cried. I knew she was trying to fail me so I would be doomed to repeat her class, but I refused to let that happen. I took an exit test to prove my language ability and passed. I went down to the registrar's office and demanded a printed copy of my test. The woman told me there was something wrong because I had two versions of the test, one pass and one fail. I told her I took only one test and passed, and she chalked it up to a mistake. Next semester, I was called down to the office to enroll in ELL or take the exit test. I reminded her that we had already talked about this before, that I had passed and was no longer in ELL. She finally remembered me and let me go back to class.

Once you're in the ELL system, it's very hard to get out. All your parents have to do when they enroll you is say you speak another language at home, and you're automatically placed, whether you're proficient or not. I also find that in ELL, you miss out on opportunities and extracurriculars that you would've been exposed to in a regular class. It's hard to advance when all you learn are simple sentences and repetition; there is no challenge.

By senior year, with graduation right around the corner, I was thinking about my future. I took part in a college readiness program called College Possible. They helped students apply for colleges and decipher FAFSA applications, and they guided us on the journey toward college. Their help made the process easier. Even still, as the eldest daughter of immigrants and the first in my family to go to college, I definitely had a lot to learn on my own. I was accepted to most schools I applied for. I ended up choosing the St. Thomas University two-year program. Even though I still remembered my ELL teacher's rude comments about college, I knew the program was the right fit for me. St. Thomas was a great school with rigorous programs. Enrolling in the two-year program all but guaranteed my acceptance into the four-year program. My time in the two-year program was remarkable. Many of my educators and peers were people of color. There was a general sense of camaraderie among the students. There was an understanding that educators were genuinely invested in the futures of their students and went above and beyond in securing opportunities.

After completing the two-year program, I was admitted into St. Thomas with a full ride. I was really happy about the acceptance and scholarship. I worked really hard to get to that position. I avoided debt as much as possible from the beginning, and my patience and careful planning paid off. The four-year program felt like another world compared to the two-year program. Most of the professors and peers were White. Most of my classmates were from the suburbs and probably came from more affluent families. I was usually one of the few Black, Muslim, or African students. I felt more alone and looked for groups to feel a sense of community on campus. In these groups, I was able to find peers I could relate to, and it made college a little less isolated. I was also able to help organize events and projects that I firmly believed in. During these years I found an interest in social work. I was always interested in helping people, and mental health is something I'm passionate about. I studied clinical social work, and now, in my final year of undergraduate studies, I'm looking forward to getting field experience. I found two practitioners with their own practices who would be willing to mentor me. I'm really excited because it's my dream to open my own clinic one day. I want to offer mental health care services to underserved communities.

～

I feel very blessed that my parents instilled the values of Islam as I was growing up. Practicing my religion in a country where I'm the minority is something I'm conscious of. For example, celebrating holidays back home is incredible. It feels like everyone is celebrating with you. You're also celebrated for excelling in Islamic studies, for being an observant Muslim. Here, you have to awkwardly ask for time off to celebrate a major Muslim holiday, and sometimes it doesn't work out when a midterm or work deadline is scheduled on Eid. It feels like your faith is an afterthought, if that. Because of the negative media depictions of

Muslims and stereotypes, it also feels like we have to be prepared to defend or explain our faith at any moment. Back home, Islam isn't this alien concept that has to be constantly analyzed and pulled apart. It's understood. I do find community in the masjid and going to dugsi. Although I've become busy with my academic studies, I really miss going to dugsi. The culture, goal setting, and group accountability helped me reach my goals and helped me stay focused and determined.

I really enjoy the general concept of intentions in Islam. Constantly setting good intentions, gaining awareness and intentionality over decision-making. Even when it comes to other people's intentions, the concept of giving people excuses, not pretending to know someone else's intentions. That only Allah (سبحانه وتعالى) knows the intentions of His creations, and it's not up to us to assume to have this intimate knowledge. I'm also motivated by the idea of doing everything for the sake of Allah (سبحانه وتعالى). In Surah Ar-Rahman, the passage lists many blessings Allah (سبحانه وتعالى) has bestowed upon us. We take a lot of those blessings for granted, and it's good to remind yourself of the mercy of our Creator. I think of gratitude most often when I am sick. Before that moment, I took my health for granted. I don't wake up every morning grateful for clear sinuses and a breath of fresh air, but I notice it most when I no longer have that blessing. It's oftentimes absence that reminds us of our own precarity and mortality.

I am Black and African, and a Somali Muslim woman. Those identities are important to me because that's how I navigate the world. It's who I belong to; it's where I get my cultural values. That's who I consider my community. I'm proud of who I am, despite what society may say. If Somalia was peaceful and developed, I would definitely go back. I consider Minnesota my residence and Somalia my home. If I did go back, I would be very happy to bring my skills and expertise and be of service to our country. I can't imagine where my family will be in one hundred years, much less five hundred years. But if I have to say, I hope they are mindful of their community, attached to their faith, and taking care of their families. I hope they are grateful for what they have and still strive to better themselves. I hope they are successful. My idea of success is being caring, contributing to society, and taking care of themselves.

I have a complex relationship with citizenship. At its most simple, I understand that to have American citizenship is an extraordinary advantage. Citizenship allows you to vote in this democracy, have rights, and be a part of society. At the same time, what's on paper doesn't translate to our cultural view of American identity. I am not perceived as American because of my race, religion, and ethnicity. We could be here for two hundred years, but we will always be seen as "hyphen-American" and not simply American. You're always foreign if you're not White. In that regard, being a citizen isn't as culturally important to me.

I'm someone who was influenced by more than one culture. In Somali culture, I really admire our sense of community, our respect for elders and deference to them.

We have kinship for one another: even as strangers we are still brothers and sisters. I also like the way we value Islam to the degree that our culture is heavily influenced by our faith. It's nice that we don't have to navigate far between our culture and faith—conflict there is minimal.

I wish we valued mothers more, especially the work of raising families and taking care of an entire household. Like other cultures, we don't respect that as much as a paycheck or bringing home money, even though being a mother is a tremendous deal of work. I also wish we had better resources for those dealing with trauma such as sexual assault, rape, and domestic violence. I think we should encourage victim survivors to seek help and better support them.

Back home, some families don't send their daughters to school because it's a financial struggle and sometimes it's not seen as valuable to educate someone who will be a housewife as opposed to someone who will earn wages. I think that idea doesn't serve the goals we have as a nation. We can't prosper as a country if half the population has barriers to education. Empowering women and girls benefits society as a whole. I also have to acknowledge it's really hard to have conversations about culture and womanhood because sincere conversations are weaponized against our communities in a bad-faith attempt to further denigrate our religion, cultures, and people. It's unfortunate because it stifles well-intentioned efforts to improve certain norms.

I believe there is a cultural gap. The younger generation is growing up in a culture very different from their parents and elders. They're taught one thing at school and another thing at home. Who should they listen to? Then kids have to pick and choose. There is good and bad in every culture. I've definitely picked as well, probably without even thinking that I was going about it that way. From Somali culture, I really appreciate the value of contentedness and gratitude no matter what your circumstance. In American culture, I'm really drawn to being an independent woman and taking care of yourself. I try to see the value of both cultures and combine perspectives.

Assimilation and integration usually make for interesting conversations. I personally am not a fan of the melting pot analogy. I think erasing or blending our differences is not necessarily needed. Let's learn from one another and appreciate each other's differences. We can all contribute to each other and work toward our shared goals

Qabil is a sensitive and hot-button issue. I think there are some good ideas about qabil, like identifying one another and kinship. But tribalism, when used to take advantage of others, to seek power, or to suggest that you're better than other people, is detrimental. I personally don't share my tribe with others because I don't want to be judged based on that. At the end of the day, we're all Somali. Let's find common ground.

⁓

My hope for Somalia is peace and prosperity. I hope young people visit Somalia in their lifetimes and know the value of our country and help rebuild and make it better. I also think young people have an advantage in not being attached to single solutions and are more open-minded at the possibilities of change—and can help be the catalysts for that change.

To Somali people:

Be proud of our culture, because there is beauty in it.

Be open-minded to change, because there is beauty in change.

Preserve your culture and make sure young people are being taught it.

Find ways to help our people back home.

To Somali girls and women:

You are resilient, intelligent, strong, and most patient. Find ways to connect with each other and empower each other. Be mindful of influences on your womanhood.

Be proud of who you are. Don't try to be anything else, because you are enough.

To Somali men and boys:

You can accomplish your goals of bettering your life, your families, and your community.

Be an active parent, because kids need their dads.

Treat the women and girls in your life with the respect they deserve. Rise to the occasion; you are capable and enough.

6

Layla Abdulkarim, 20s, Middle East

pseudonym

I was born in Kuwait. We moved to Minnesota when I was young. I joke that my parents still thought we were nomadic in America, because it seems like we've always been on the move. We've lived in the metro, in the suburbs, and in rural towns. Always on the search for something better.

I've been blessed to have both my parents in my life. I am a middle child of ten children and the eldest girl. But I may as well be the eldest child, with the amount of responsibility I've had since a young age. I was a middle child with no middle-child advantages. Only the burden of the eldest and none of the youngest sibling perks.

I am the first daughter born to my mother. She tried for years to have a girl and instead bore five sons. I was then the first of five subsequent daughters. My mother was at first hopelessly outnumbered. She reminisces that when she found out she was pregnant with a girl, she often said she wouldn't mind being pregnant with me forever.

When I was still relatively new to this country, I didn't know the language well enough to communicate. One day, a class-mate's packed lunch went missing. Our teacher was determined to get to the bottom of it. I wasn't stupid; I just didn't know how to say, "I didn't do it." The only other Somali girl in the class spoke English fluently. Without even flinching, she told our teacher that she saw me steal it. I couldn't believe my eyes. Our teacher scolded me, and all I could feel was rage and helplessness. I knew what I wanted to say, but they wouldn't understand me; per-haps they wouldn't even believe me. The girl later recanted her accusation and admitted that she was the lunchtime bandit. But it was too late. I was embarrassingly aware that my fate was in the hands of a heartless second grader. This is one of my earliest memories of America. I'm not sure why I remember it so vividly. Perhaps it is because of my Somali girl superpower: the ability to sense unfairness and be profoundly repulsed by it.

~

Every Somali girl knows the eldest daughter's burden. It's no secret that we wear many hats. We are the second or third parents, cooks, housekeepers, accountants, doctors, therapists, lawyers, chauffeurs, and everything in between. We have to grow up early because our parents need our help and our siblings need us. It's often a thankless and invisible job, but behind every household there's usually at least one daughter manning the fort. As a community, we often talk about the benefits of raising our daughters in a guarded way, with many responsibilities at an early age, but I don't think we acknowledge the consequences. It's really easy to see the success, accolades, and achievements of women and girls, but we don't acknowledge the turmoil and trauma they could've been spared. Depriving someone of their childhood isn't noble; it can lead to resentment, burnout, and undue struggle.

Girls are expected to do it all and have it all. It's a tremendous amount of pressure that has its benefits and drawbacks as well. A lot of people can easily identify the successes of this cultural rearing method. Somali girls are known for excelling in their education and careers, all while raising their families. The outward and observable successes are what people pick up on, without noticing the issues and dangers. When boys act out, there is usually a noticeable behavioral shift that is external. When girls act out, it can go under the radar if one isn't looking. A lot of girls are dealing with mental health issues, stress, or identity issues, and these problems aren't dealt with by parents until it's past a certain point. Or the problems are even discounted. We might hear, "What reason do you have to be depressed or anxious? You have it easy compared to us." Parents can overlook the problems their kids experience in this culture and time because of the weight of issues they experienced growing up back home. But ignoring a problem or downplaying it doesn't address the issue at hand. Girls are good at hiding their issues because there is an expectation of what is acceptable and a fear of mistakes. So instead of seeking help, some girls will struggle alone and hide it from their parents or family.

I discovered the biggest barrier to my education close to my undergraduate commencement. I found out I had a learning disability. This made a lot of sense. It took me longer to complete assignments, assessments, and projects. As a child, I excelled at math and science but had some difficulty with reading. Teachers just attributed this to being an ESL student and not an underlying issue. They would remark on my report cards some words about having potential but struggling with attention and time management.

It was right there for my educators or parents to see, but no one picked up on it. I just flew under the radar. That's the problem with not being a problem child or extrovert. No one notices when you're struggling because the struggle is internal. It's subtle. Gaining a sense of self-understanding and asking for accommodations made a world of difference in my studies when I was properly diagnosed. I couldn't help but think, *Where would I be if I had known earlier?*

When I was in high school, I enrolled in courses at my local community college. Taking those college-level courses allowed me to gain credit to go toward a degree. My counselor heavily discouraged me and did not help through the process. My mom and I fought about taking those college classes too. She thought I was too young to start college and it was too dangerous for me to be in the big, scary city by myself. She would rather I stick to what I know. My dad was ambivalent and eventually got behind it. I had to fight to get there, but I refused to give up. My thing is that no one can tell me I can't do something. I will do it just to prove them wrong.

When you're a child of immigrants, you spend a lot of time figuring things out for yourself. In the same way I applied for college courses in high school, the time came for me to apply to college. The SAT, applications, FAFSA—this was a whole new world for me. Luckily, I had the help of our college resource person, Ms. Bark. She was beloved by everyone but especially students who didn't have resources about college. She was a petite White woman with smile lines that remained long after she stopped smiling. Ms. Bark made our dreams her own. She was our school mom. Ms. Bark helped pick out schools and prep for the SAT, let us loiter in the career department between classes, wrote God-knows-how-many recommendation letters, and always offered a smile and word of encouragement. That woman could do no wrong. She did for generations too. Everyone knew that Ms. Bark was on our side.

My path to college was unpredictable. After graduating from high school, I enrolled in a private college. None of my friends were attending this college, and so I was pretty lonely being a new student. Tuition was very expensive, and I struggled to afford it. I also didn't drive or have a car, so I had to take three buses starting at 6:00 in the morning to arrive in time for my 8:00 AM class. I even enrolled in a class at a different university and commuted between campuses. I was a biology major in a school not known for its biology program. I flunked most of my classes that semester. My time there was an uphill struggle. So why was I there? I felt this tremendous pressure to go to a four-year university. I wanted to make my parents proud and keep up with my friends who were going to another school.

There is a stigma against community college. People might assume you weren't smart or ambitious enough to go straight to a four-year. But this simply isn't true. Most eighteen-year-olds can't tell you what they're having for lunch, much less what they will be doing professionally in five years, so why do we expect them to go tens or hundreds of thousands of dollars into debt for a career path they might not follow? Time is the most valuable asset for a student. They need time to figure out what they want to do, what they're good at, to find the perfect sweet spot between the two. Community college is an affordable way to buy that time.

The general credits a student needs at a four-year accredited institution are usually the same at a community college, but at a much less expensive rate. Community college isn't an option for everyone, but it's an option everyone should consider, especially if the burden of tuition is a barrier, as it is for most Americans. Looking back, I wish I had examined the anxiety I felt toward higher education and not allowed the expectations of others to drive my decisions. My path was not going to be the same as everyone else's; the sooner I realized that, the easier things would be for me.

My friends were graduating college before me, and it had me feeling some type of way. I felt inadequate and doubtful about my journey. Was I doing the right thing? Was I in the right field? Would this be worth the risk? I felt this underlying uneasiness for months without acknowledging the tremendous pressure I was under and the feeling of loss and uncertainty I felt at watching my friends reach this milestone without me. I had to confront these feelings and address the emotions that had been brewing up inside of me. I realized then that I had no right to compare myself to anyone. I did not bear the journey of my peers, nor they mine.

I was a biology major because I was going into medicine. My parents always wanted me to be a doctor, and I wanted to be in the medical field. I worked toward becoming a physician's assistant or PA. I left private college after one semester and enrolled at a community college. I really enjoyed my time there. The classes and teachers were diverse, and I got there with one bus. After community college, I transferred to a bigger college. During these semesters, I took a lot of biology and sciences classes. Chemistry was my archnemesis. I took chemistry over and over again, because even though it sucked, I needed it for my degree. I was determined to pursue it at all costs. I failed that class six times in multiple schools. I refused to give up despite the giant stop sign in front of me. If there wasn't a way for me, I would make my way.

During my time at this college, I met another Somali girl who was a STEM major with a focus in mathematics. I never even heard of this degree, let alone considered that as a career option. But it made sense to me because I enjoyed problem-solving, math, science, logic, and reasoning. And even though I was intimidated, I was also intrigued.

I signed up for a mathematics class that semester. And I failed miserably. Even though I went to a tutor almost every single day and asked for help, I still tanked. I would ask, "How do you this? How do you compute this? How do you do that?" And at that moment I said to myself, *Okay. This is what I'm going to do the rest of my life.* Why? I'm not entirely sure. Perhaps it was the challenge, the way things just made sense, and the way it fit into my life like a missing puzzle piece. This was for me; I knew it in my bones. I couldn't have gotten higher than a D, but if I could fail chemistry six times, then at least I could fail something I was beginning to love.

I was almost done with my biology degree when I completely switched majors to mathematics. To say this was a bold move would be an understatement. This decision shocked my parents. My academic advisors recommended against changing majors when I was so close to finishing my biology degree. My friends wondered if I was having a premature midlife crisis. It was such a huge leap of faith, but I knew deep down that this was the right thing for me. Sometimes you have to be willing to bet on yourself, even when the odds might not be in your favor.

Higher education was the best educational experience that I had. Finally, I had a chance to challenge myself and be independent. I made many mistakes, but I was so excited to make decisions and own the outcome, negative or positive. It would be my choice.

I can't really recall any grade school or high school teachers who stick out in my mind as having a profound impact on me, but this is where college changed everything. At my final school, I had a tight-knit community of teachers, advisers, and department staff. These people took a genuine interest in me and my education. I had teachers recommend internships and an advisor meet with me to recommend me for a scholarship. There was a level of sincere support I was unaccustomed to up until that point. I didn't feel like I was doing this by myself anymore. I felt like there were people on campus who genuinely had my back, and it was the push I needed to keep me going after all the upsets.

This last leg of my education was not without its challenges. Tuition for a private university was very expensive. Financial aid covered a portion of the cost, but I was responsible for the rest. I worked at a small office overnights and weekends to pay what I could and had the blessing of my family to lean on when I needed it. I had no life but school. Clocking into work would serve as a regular reminder for why this school thing needed to pay off in the end, because I could not be stuck working a job like that for the rest of my life. Eventually I was able to find internships that were relevant to my courses, thanks to my supportive instructors and advisors. At one point I was taking classes full-time and working two part-time internships. I was on top of my game. I felt great because I was being so productive and working toward my dreams. Things were finally going in the right direction.

~

Image and reputation are really important to Somali culture. Part of that makes sense: you're only as good as your word, and what people think of you in a communal society matters. But other parts of it are circular in reasoning. For example, my siblings and I hated hearing "How would that look?" Our parents ended arguments with their ultimate trump card: "No, because how would that look?" It was not simply that we couldn't afford X or no one had time to take us to Y but that we had to worry about the way it would look to other people. This baffled my siblings because someone else's judgments hardly seemed like a barrier to our plans. We were even more infuriated when criticisms magically tied back to marriage. If we couldn't muster the will to cook or to clean the carpet just right, how could we hope to keep a man? If we can't pick up after everyone, what if we got sent back like a defective can opener with a factory warranty? I knew early on there was a double standard in our home between my brothers and my sisters. The girls were responsible for the large majority of chores. Every once in a while my mom would try to get our brothers to chip in, but they were too set in their ways, and no one had the energy to reorient them.

Sometime after college, I started going to therapy. I went because I was going through a lot of changes in life and the chaos of it all begin to peel back thoughts and behaviors I wanted to examine. I had created a new normal without consciously thinking about what I was doing. College was a stressful period in my life that led me to develop my own unhealthy coping mechanisms. I had to reconsider thought patterns and habits and see things from a new point of view. I had to consciously decide to not let the way other people think influence me. That means being intentional about who I surround myself with.

Therapy wasn't just about self-image and habits. I also had to deal with hard realities. Ever since I was a kid, I played the peacemaker role between my siblings and parents. I understood where everyone was coming from and didn't want to see conflict. I made it my job to help resolve conflict and keep the peace in the household. It was such a stressful role and a burden to carry. One day my brother pulled me to the side and said that I didn't *have* to be the peacemaker. I realized he was right and resigned from the self-appointed role. I was no longer responsible for the relationships between other people, and it was the most freeing thing ever. How could I ever control that? I can only control myself, and the sooner I realized that, the better.

It wasn't just the peacemaker role. I also learned early on to keep my opinions and emotions to myself. Whenever I got expressive defending myself or sharing my opinions, my parents would chastise me for being emotional. Their response taught me to shrink into myself. Be agreeable. Go with everyone else's ideas before my own. Keep the peace. This way of living built a quiet resentment and a dull anger inside me. I didn't have a voice. Or rather, I had a voice, but no one seemed to listen. It occurred to me that minimizing myself was just a way of stopping others from hurting me. I didn't have to face rejection if I rejected myself, right? But this was no way to live, not meaningfully at least. In order to change, I had to learn to speak up for myself even when no one would hear me.

～

I love my parents. I'm grateful I had them to raise me and look out for me. The best lessons they taught me were through their actions. Both of my parents are hustlers. My mom started a business out of her car, moved it to our apartment, and eventually opened an office, all on her own. She brought us to a country where she did not know the language, customs, or traditions and made a way for herself so she could provide for us. I can't imagine doing a tenth of what she's done. My mom loves hard, and her loyalty can never be doubted.

My dad is our entire family's coach, advisor, and cheerleader. He encouraged my siblings to go back to school, start businesses, and create legacies. He's always thinking of his family back home and how to get them out of poverty and educated and to become entrepreneurs. He's ten steps ahead of everyone, thinking of how each person can reach their full potential and how to support them. Even when my mom pushed back against my ideas for my education or goals out of fear for me, my dad would back me on them. He believed in me. The older I get, the more grateful I am for their roles in my life, flaws and all. I can truly say without a shadow of a doubt that they tried their best and that they wanted the best for me.

Parents are not perfect, that much we can all agree on. When you're a kid, you think your parents are superheroes. Only when you get older do you realize how ordinary they really are. They have money problems, bad habits, biases, baggage, trauma, and fears. They had lives long before us. Parents can't give what they don't have. Sometimes being a parent can bring out the best in someone or expose their underlying issues. Having empathy and understanding for your parents is life-shifting. Forgiving someone even when you'll never get an apology is okay because forgiveness is for you. It allows you to acknowledge and heal from past harm. At some point, we're all accountable for ourselves, and we choose what types of lives we want to lead. It's up to us to break the cycles of trauma, violence, and abuse in our families. It starts with us. That is an extraordinary task, but in the same way people can be taught to hurt others, we can teach each other to love, be gentle, and heal our pain. We are capable of that, through the mercy of God.

Friendships are so important to me. My girls got me through a lot of things and have lent their strength and love when I needed it. I don't know where I'd be without my tribe. It made me realize the type of friends I want to have and also the type of friend I want to be. I want to be there for them, love them, celebrate them, go through the hard times and be their rock, set them straight when they need it, and cherish them. I'm actually better for it, because it made me more conscious of the quality of my friendships and to actively breathe life into them.

～

Islam has been an integral part of my life. I always went to dugsi, but we moved around so much we never set down roots. We focused on recitation and memorization, but in hindsight I wish we had also focused on history, seerah, and tazkiya and other parts of our rich faith tradition. When I grew up, I reconnected to my faith in a more active role, as opposed to being a passenger. It helped me appreciate the beauty of Islam and gave me a chance to discover it in a way I wasn't taught. The lessons of mercy, forgiveness, and love have really touched my heart. My parents always instilled the values of faith in our lives. They were role models in the sense that they themselves practiced what they preached and led by example. They also leaned on the fear and consequence aspects of religion. I would have appreciated being taught to do things for the pleasure of Allah (سبحانه وتعالى). Fear-based teaching is a one-dimensional interpretation of Allah (سبحانه وتعالى) and His religion. I find that beauty and gentleness resonate with me better. The calmness they bring to my life is so motivating and inspiring. There's definitely more than one way to instill those values, and I hope to lead by example with my own kids one day.

I am a Black Somali Muslim woman. Those identities helped shape the person I am. When I was younger, two students interviewed me in a class project on heritage. They asked, "What are you?" I was born in the Middle East, lived in Europe, and immigrated to the States early on—and grew up in American culture and was of Somali descent. So what does that make me? I said I identify as Somali, and they asked, "Why? Have you been there?" I said no, and they asked what made me identify as Somali. I said because that's who I am. That's the language I speak, the food I eat, the culture I live, and the person I am without ever having taken a step on the continent. My identity transcends time and space. I am who I am.

I am most of aware of being a Black woman or a Somali as a data analyst. It's been rare to see someone who looks like me in my career. I get so excited when I see my peers at conferences or when a new person joins the office. There's an instant understanding of communal experience and camaraderie that I love. As a woman in tech, I'm keenly aware of the need to be prepared to defend my decisions and share my ideas, even when it's not easy. I know that my role in this field is to solve interesting problems and encourage young women to make their way.

I know I am an American, legally and by geography, but it's hard to identify that way. I've lived here for the majority of my life, I've consumed American culture and food, and this is where I grew up—yet it's hard to name it as my home. If you disagree with American politics or make a comment on American culture, you're immediately barraged with insults and calls to "go back home" or "go back to Africa." In Somali culture, no matter how flagrant your belief, you're still Somali. It's not a revokable card when people disagree with you. I'm not sure if this happens in other countries or if it's racialized like this across the world. If I travel internationally, I would definitely identify as an American. But it feels like a stretch to call myself American without being called on to do so.

I'd love to visit Somalia, but I don't plan on living anywhere else. I think about growing up back home if the war hadn't happened. What kind of life would I be living? Would I be married? Have kids? I'm not sure, but it would definitely be different. I don't know where my family will be in a hundred years. I can't imagine my ancestors thought we would be where we are today. I hope our country is safe and that my descendants have the option to live there. In five hundred years, I can only hope that we're still Muslim. I can't ask for anything beyond that.

I had no business being in the relationships I've been in. For the record, my parents never pushed marriage on me. They never try to set me up or pressure me to get married. They trusted that I would bring the right person home and made clear what they wanted in a partner for me. So I figured things out for myself.

And I found a pattern in my relationships. I was insecure about myself. I was looking for the wrong things in the wrong people at the wrong time. God has always protected me. I didn't know what I wanted, what to put up with, and what to expect. Now I'm clear and I wouldn't tolerate 99 percent of the nonsense I did. Ladies, be intentional and be clear.

Over the years, I've learned to always reflect and be willing to grow. The most painful parts of my life have shaped me to be stronger and have more empathy for others. God truly does not test you with more than you can handle. I've also learned to speak up for myself, because no one else will. To be accountable to yourself. To not rely on anyone else to make your happiness. I am in control of only a tiny portion of my life; I cannot control the outcome or a million other factors. That is freeing knowledge and a reminder that I am not in control; only God is. I am responsible for a small part, and the rest I leave to my Creator.

∾

To my Somali sisters, your families and our society do not define who you are. Don't let anyone tell you about yourself. Go find out for yourself. To my Somali brothers, take care of your friends and family, the ones you love. Nobody ever moves by themselves in this world; there are a lot of people counting on you. Do good for yourself. To my people, keep up the good fight. Don't give up on each other. Keep our country and our people in your hearts. Keep the love. Salaam each other. Be a peace to one another.

7

Amran Farah, 30s, Mogadishu, Somalia

I was born in Xamar, Somalia. I am a middle child, number seven of eleven to be exact. I come from a big family. Like a classic middle child, I was an overachiever. I had to be outstanding in something.

I was young when the war broke out, and we fled Somalia and came to the States. We ended up in San Diego, where we stayed for some years before heading to the Midwest. When we moved to Minnesota, that was the first time we saw snow. Before that, we had seen snow only in movies and TV shows. The novelty wore off faster than you'd expect.

Our parents had their lives before America. Mom came from a well-off family, and Dad came from a well-educated, middle-class family. My mom's family thought she could do better and wanted her to marry someone richer, but eventually they got married. My mom was a community health worker and doula back home. She never lets me forget I nearly killed her during my birth. I was a breech baby, and the doctors wanted to deliver me via C-section. My mother refused despite the risk of death if the labor continued. Still, she was adamant. One doctor made a last attempt to deliver me safely and tried to physically flip me by pressing on my mother's belly. It didn't work. Finally, I rotated myself and was delivered without a C-section. For that reason, my parents named me Amran, because it was only by amarka illahi that I was born safely.

I remember the Civil War in bursts. Growing up, I heard so many stories from my siblings that their stories have fused into my memories. The war erupted quickly. Luckily, because of my parents' station, we were able to get out just as fast as it had started. My uncle was a pilot, and we stayed in his Nairobi home for a while. Then we stayed with our grandfather in Mombasa. Finally, we were granted asylum in the United States. There was a long journey before this, however. When we applied for asylum initially, we were granted it by the British government. However, not all of us would be able to go. We would have to leave my brother behind. My parents made the decision to decline the offer because they believed strongly that we needed to stay together as a family. Our relatives told us to take the offer and sponsor my brother later; it was no big deal; people did it all the time to survive. But my parents refused. If we were going to leave, we would leave together. No one gets left behind.

I always wonder what life would've been like if the war hadn't happened. I think I would have gotten married sooner, and I hope I could have an education like I do now, but I don't know if that would've happened. I want to go back one day to visit. I've made so many plans to visit, but they always get ruined. Once my mother and I had planned a trip, and on the day we were supposed to go, my mother fell ill and we had to cancel. I jokingly say that maybe Malak al-mawt is waiting for me there, and maybe that's why my plans to visit keep failing.

My dad was a math teacher and the strongest advocate for education you'd ever meet. When we were kids, we hated getting in trouble in front of our dad. When teachers at school or dugsi would criticize or complain about us, our mom always took up for us. She would empathize with our busy schedules and schoolwork. "Maybe they've had a hard week," she would say in our defense. Our father was the opposite. He would always take the side of our teachers. "What did he do? Sounds just like him!" One time, my brother naively complained to Dad about a teacher who didn't like him. "Why would your teacher dislike you? You're insignificant. You are one of many. And if she doesn't like you, what did you do to make her dislike you?"

He didn't like to hear excuses from us because he knew that our educations were the keys to our futures. He was our disciplinarian. Even worse from the viewpoint of a kid, he was our teacher outside of school. He refused to let us use calculators until later in school. Instead, he would assign long division and times tables to us during our free time. He was passionate about valuing our diin and dhaqan, so in addition to dugsi, he taught us how to read and write in Somali script. From what I heard from my friends, this was not typical. We were excellent students because we had no choice. If we complained about school, he would ask, "Do you have a job? What else do you possibly have going on?"

My dad didn't believe in welfare. He said the system was designed to keep you on it for the rest of your life. He was the provider in our household and worked very hard to support his family. Because of my profession as a lawyer, my dad and I are really close. I was one of the kids who really listened to him and pursued my education strongly, early on. Out of all my siblings, I'm the one who embraced his ideology on education. I read as much as my dad does. Even now, he sends me books, and we have interesting conversations about life and the world around us. He secretly had hoped I would be a writer like my uncle, but I'm not.

My mom and I are best friends. We were always close when I was growing up. My mom was our champion and my confidante. Back home she was in health care, and she became a traditional homemaker when we got to the States. We talk at least once a day and vacation together. When the kids grew up, my parents sold their home. My dad started heading back home for the winters, and I bought my mom a townhome. I don't brag, but it's well known that I am her favorite. After all, I've earned it.

My dad was deferential to my mom in the home. She decided where we'd move and what furniture we had. My dad had old-school ideas on roles. The home was her domain. When we were in Somalia, she had a nanny and a maid as well as her family to help her. When we got to the States, the older kids were helping around the house and helping look after the younger kids. So she wasn't always on her own.

My parents stressed the importance of family. My siblings and I are super close. We've got a group chat that keeps us up to date on all the family news. If I texted the group right now that I need a ride somewhere, someone will be here within an hour. We have a tradition of each pitching in $1,000 every time someone gets married so we can bless them with a gift. We know that we can rely on each other. When my dad got sick and needed heart surgery during COVID, the medical staff would allow only one person a day to stay with him. We set up a calendar and assumed shifts so he always had someone by his side. We look out for each other because our parents taught us family is everything. They showed us love through acts of service.

We had typical gender roles growing up. The boys weren't expected to help around the house. But my older sister forced the younger brothers to help out, just like their sisters. At the same time, our parents expected all of us to go to college and not get married at fifteen. They had high expectations for all of their kids. One thing I wish we would have gotten to do was travel together as a family. We couldn't afford it. I know before we came to the States, my parents would travel to places like Egypt and Tanzania. But in America, we were poor. We never felt poor, though; our parents sheltered us from poverty.

⁓

I went to elementary school in San Diego and grew up with Black friends. We moved to Minneapolis by middle school. I attended Sanford Middle School, where I made Somali friends who were authentically Somali. My friends had recently arrived in the States, they wore khamaar unlike myself, and they helped me bloom my own Somali identity. Eventually, I went to Roosevelt High School, known as Little Mogadishu because of the number of Somali students. Growing up, I had African American friends and eventually Somali friends when we came to Minnesota. Our father was a strong Pan-Africanist, and I shared his affinity for all of our people. At the end of the day, we are Black, he would say. He stressed how in this country, our closest brothers were Black Americans. At Roosevelt, I saw that this sentiment was not largely shared by either African American students or Somali students. This idea that we're all Black and kin was not widely accepted. But I kicked it with everyone. I loved Roosevelt and the Black and Somali friends I made because they were a little bit of all my identities combined.

I was an overachiever. I received high marks, top of my class, was in the National Honor Society. High school was a blast for me. I was voted best dressed and was voted Snow Days Queen. I brag, but high school was fun for me.

Because I did so well in school, my dad rarely had any reason to check up on me. The only time he came to the campus was when I was put in an interactive math program class. In this class, they taught math by words rather than numbers. My dad went to my counselor and told her to switch me to regular geometry. His excuse for switching me was that he needed to help me and he didn't understand teaching geometry through word problems. The counselor politely told him that I had an A in the class and didn't need the extra tutoring.

The coolest thing about Roosevelt was that I had a class called "Somali for Somali Speakers," taught by the famous poet, writer, professor, and academic Macalin Said Salah himself. It was the most entertaining class by far. We were always laughing or having fun. I knew how to read and write already because of my dad. Our first assignment was to learn a Somali proverb and explain it in Somali and in English. We would go up to the FOBs and ask them to teach us. The problem was, they would only teach us the nasty mahmahs that would make us blush.

We would learn about different names for grass and livestock. I still can't tell you the different names between sheep and lambs. This class was a great chance to learn more about Somali culture and language.

The biggest challenge I faced in school was the lowered expectations of my teachers and administrators. Because I was an immigrant kid, they expected me to fail. If I did even remotely well, I would get so much credit at school because they expected the bare minimum. But at home, my dad wouldn't accept anything but excellence. The school gave me so many excuses for my imminent failure. For example, in middle school, when we were reading a book aloud in class, a substitute teacher told me I didn't have to read and skipped me. I was an excellent reader but also a kid who didn't want to do more work, so I was okay with that.

When we struggled or complained about how hard school was, my dad would threaten to send us back to Somalia and exchange us for a grateful kid who didn't whine about the breadth of opportunity they were given. We called his bluff when we figured out no Somali kid would want to be standing in the Minnesota cold at a bus stop at 6:00 in the morning.

In high school, I was in a program called Admissions Possible, now called College Possible. I was in a group with White kids and three other Somalis. Our advisor was a Somali guy who went to Hamline University. His name is Abdi. We stayed in touch for many years. He was a humble guy who showed us a lot of kindness. Just like my dad, he refused to let us fail. He went above and beyond for his Somali kids. For one of his students, he would drive to his house, wake him up, and drive him to ACT prep class. He didn't want to hear any excuses from us. He would stress that he would make sure the other kids were straight, but he needed us to win. Some other Somali students didn't want to ask him for help on college stuff and instead went to the White advisors. They had no idea what it was like to have a guy like Abdi in your corner.

I remember one time he made us give him our college statements so he could review them. He told one kid, "You, lessen your calaacal. All you do is complain—talk about your academic achievements and merit." Then he turned to me. "You, you don't calaacal enough. If I read this statement, I would think you were a White girl from the suburbs of Minneapolis. Talk about being an immigrant, Somali, Blackness, whatever. But show how your identity impacted or shaped you." I still remembered his advice in law school. I remembered his theory on balance, to not go too heavy to one side or another, to instead tell a well-rounded view of a story. I was awarded many scholarships in college, and I have to credit Abdi.

We wanted to apply to a school or two, but Abdi made us apply to five schools each. I knew I was gonna go to the University of Minnesota. Everyone I knew went to the U—my siblings, my friends—and I was even attending PSEO at the U during that time. But Abdi insisted. So I took school tours at Gustavus, Hamline, St. Thomas, the University of Minnesota, and Augsburg. I got a full scholarship to St. Thomas, and Abdi encouraged me to go there. I never would've heard of St. Thomas if Abdi hadn't forced me to apply to five schools.

~

I went to St. Thomas to study premed and chemistry. I took a logic class and fell in love with it. This led me to law. I went to Hamline for law school and eventually took my bar exam. I re- member the day of the test. It was Ramadan, and I had been fasting all day. The exam takes two days to finish. I prayed that I would pass. I didn't break my fast. I thought to myself, what a colossal waste if I broke my fast only to fail the exam. I passed. At the time, I didn't know you were supposed to look for intern- ships for the summer, starting the year before. So I scrambled to find an internship the spring before summer break. I found something eventually, but I'm very aware of not having a blue- print for my education and career. I didn't always have mentors or people who could tell me XYZ to accomplish my goals. I had to navigate a new world all on my own. That comes with making mistakes and continuing anyway.

I got married. I worked for the Hennepin County prosecu- tor's office. Eventually, I was asked to join the good side and went on to clerk for the public defender's office. I received a scholarship to intern for Judge Michael Davis. He then referred me to his friend and colleague Judge Pamela Alexander.

Judge Pamela Alexander is a well-known judge. In the nine- ties, she was nominated by Senator Paul Wellstone for the fed- eral bench, one of the most prestigious ranks in the courts. In *State v. Russell*, she noted the discrepancies in sentencing be- tween powder cocaine and crack cocaine. She identified the ra- cial components of those unfair sentences. Because she spoke up, she received a lot of criticism from those who were worried she would be an activist judge. She eventually withdrew her nomination. Many years later, it's acknowledged that Judge Al- exander was simply ahead of her time and not afraid to be right. In working with her, I've come to personally admire her unapol- ogetic and principled nature.

She shared a story with me about her time in Ghana. When

she arrived in Ghana with other judges for an event, the local Ghanaians were shocked to see her. They said how can someone like you with hair like that be an important person in America? The judge wore her hair naturally. They expected to see someone with relaxer or extensions. And even though how anyone wears their hair is their own business, we're also role models for how others are shaping themselves. It reminded me about the power of being authentically myself. When you are authentic, others who look up to you will gain the confidence to also be themselves. Besides my son, my greatest accomplishments are my career and education, as well as the way I have intentionally stayed true to who I am.

I worked for a private firm for a bit. I was told early on I would do a lot of learning on the go and not have my hand held through the process. I hit the ground running, and I learned a lot. Eventually, I considered where I wanted my career to go. After having done criminal defense, I found I wanted to do civil court. I knew that if I waited too long in my career, I would be pigeonholed to criminal. I took a leap of faith and ended up at my current firm, Greene Espel, a litigation boutique. Power structures in the legal industry are often hierarchal. There's an order of power based on title and length of time at that office. I was dubious at first about joining the firm because the guy who recruited me went to Yale for undergrad and law school. I looked at their lineup online, and it was filled with Ivy League alumni. We didn't have the same pedigree. I would also be the only Black and only Muslim lawyer. I remember telling a friend, "I'm gonna mess up their lineup." It ended up being the best career decision I made. This firm respects me and the work I do. I had a client once who used the n-word during a meeting. I stopped the meeting and corrected him. In some places, you can't do that. You have to leave your identity and self-respect at home.

Becoming a managing partner at my firm was a huge milestone in my career. Even being considered is a huge deal. This was happening in the midst of a tumultuous year, when I was on maternity leave for four months, during the pandemic, during the George Floyd protests. It was a very hard decision to make. I was in an unstable place. I had to talk to my colleagues and family as well as do some soul-searching. Did I want to postpone the consideration because it was a hard year or because—deep down—I didn't feel good enough? I have to credit my partnership review team for making me feel so comfortable with the process. We talked about the narrative of how I wanted my partnership review to go. I did a ton of research on experiences of Black women lawyers during their partnership reviews. The deciding factor wasn't always the actual vote but instead how the women were perceived. The narrative might be either "Oh, she's not ready of course, but we took a chance on her" or "We know she's a hard worker, but is she really gonna bring in clients?" I'm grateful to the firm because I know that no other place would have really listened to my concerns about the process.

They've done this in other ways too. Sometimes I close my office door because I'm praying and need privacy and time. Or I'll request a meeting time or call be changed because it conflicts with my prayer time. During Ramadan, I change my schedule so I can fast and observe worship comfortably. Being able to practice my faith and be myself has taken away a lot of anxiety about being a Black Muslim woman at a firm. I get to be myself and do my job. I know that's not something everyone has to think about, but it goes a long way for those who do.

I've worn a lot of different hats in the legal community. I was the first president of the Somali Bar Association. That role taught me a lot about myself and my community. The organization came about as a way for Somali lawyers in North America to connect with one another. It was a place for us to build camaraderie and network professionally. I'm someone who is goal oriented and works with the intention of executing our objectives. As a woman in a leadership role, I experienced the stigma of being perceived as domineering. I also realized I differed from some people in our reactions to being the "first." In minority communities, there is always going to be the "first" anyone breaking down a barrier in any industry. For some, there is pride in being a pioneer, and they celebrate holding that title. For me and others, it reminds us of how far we have to go, as well as the barriers in the industry for people based on identity. In 2020, we shouldn't be excessively proud to be the first "Black" or "Somali" or "woman" anything—it should remind us of the racial or class-based inequities that are still very much part of the fabric of our society.

I'm also the president of MABL, the Minnesota Association of Black Lawyers. I was a new mom reeling from the murder of George Floyd and subsequent protests for Black lives, during COVID-19, but in spite of it all I had to get back to work. We prepared a statement and organized. My hope for the Somali Bar Association was to create formal structures, similar to older organizations like MABL. I was unfortunately burned out from attempts to formalize the organization, as was Aliyah, another lawyer at SBA who worked closely with me. We loved the events we held, such as a Know Your Rights training at the Brian Coyle Center. For us, our skills were only as good as what we could do for our community.

～

Back home, our families had social capital. We could influence law, culture, and the ways people lived. We gave that up in order to find opportunity in this country. Regardless of how hard you work in life, what determines your opportunities and influence is social capital, either yours or your family's. That social capital is how legacy kids get into Harvard and Yale, what gets someone a job at the mayor's office, and ultimately who determines the laws that impact everyday people. As busy as I am as a mom, wife, and managing partner at a law firm, I still do my best to be a part of organizations and movements. The reason I'm so involved is because I have to build social capital. You have to have social capital in order to create real change. Some people think this means getting a job at an institution and changing it from the inside. But more times than not, the institution eats that person, because that's what it was created to do. We all have to determine for ourselves how we go about building social capital and how we use it to make change. For me, it means holding political office or trying to change a harmful institution from the inside. I want to build influence so that I may stop the people who are inherently bad for our communities from wielding power against us.

Gatekeeping is an essential part of keeping out those who are just going to sell our people to the highest bidder. If we don't build internal structures in our communities to keep bad-faith agents out, we allow them to dominate and abuse their responsibilities to the people they should be serving. For example, in my role as president of MABL, I've done a lot of interfacing for the judicial selection committee for the state and governor. I care deeply about who gets to be a judge because that role holds a lot of power in people's lives, like in sentence disparities. I've had the privilege of working with a judge who really cares about sentencing and understands what 120 months means to a family. Can that be said about every judge? And if not, should they be in the position to make such an important decision in a family's life? Who we vote into those offices matters, and we need to be able to make the right decisions in order to advocate for our communities and the world we want to live in.

Along the way, I've discovered the reaction to successful women in our culture. There is a subtle expectation from the older generation that the more educated and successful a woman becomes, the more likely people are to expect her to remove her hijab in order to fit in better, whereas the younger generation is prouder to be different and sort of cling on tighter to their markers of cultural identity. To some, this may be the opposite of their assumptions. But I think young people are prouder because they've grown up here in this American culture and therefore appreciate the history of race and identity in this country in a different way. Because of this, I'm also conscious about whom I represent simply by looking the way I do. Therefore, I am intentional about not erasing myself or minimizing my culture and faith, because I know that someone has to open that door first. It will be easier for people down the road to remain true to who they are if the first ones opening doors do so with them in mind. For example, any time I take office pictures or do events for the firm, I always wear my hijab down fully. I could easily wrap my hair in a turban and be super chic, but I want to be a hijabi, not a turbanista. I want to be fully myself, not just someone who is more palatable to others.

How we experience marriage and motherhood is also different from previous generations. Our generation is taking longer to have kids and having fewer kids. This is for many reasons. For me, when I married my husband, I received a lot of pressure to have kids immediately. I wanted to take a year to get to know him. My dad is very politically correct. He would casually say, "It's nice to have kids younger, because you get to experience the world with your children." My mom was less strategic and would frustratingly say, "He's your husband: what else do you need to know? People get married and have kids the next day." Other people blamed my career. Our generation is doing things differently; not badly, just differently. Do what works for you.

～

My dad was hit the hardest in our family by the COVID restrictions. Normally, he travels to Kismaayo when the weather gets cold in Minnesota. But he was stuck because of the lockdown. Because he was trapped at home for weeks, his energy was low, and I suspected he was depressed. Once he left, his mood and health improved. Kismaayo is special to my dad. His sister used to work for UNICEF when she was killed in a terror attack. My dad and his siblings pitched in money to build a masjid in her name. He goes back to manage it. Because he's retired, it keeps him busy and moving around. It's something for him to work on, especially because it's special to him. I can only imagine how painful it was being away from it, not knowing when or if he'd be back.

I was pregnant before coronavirus hit the States. I had already begun working from home, and I had my son during the second month of lockdown. My mom moved in with us to look after me. What was the hardest at this point was the isolation from my friends and family. The birth was hard because I was not allowed to have more than one person with me for the delivery. I will carry to my grave who I picked to stay with me. Afterward, I wasn't allowed to have guests. This was tough because I have been to each and every one of my nieces' and nephews' births. After that, people weren't allowed to visit me when I came home. To this day, I have friends who have never seen my son. I have friends and family who bought him baby gifts and were never able to give them to him. By now, he's grown out of the gifts they bought.

One blessing I cannot stress enough is how amazingly my job supported me. I was granted four-month parental leave with full salary. I didn't have to worry about losing my job or making ends meet. My mother and husband were with me every step of the way. One of my sisters who lived with my mom was in our bubble, and I could at least see her. I had some of my support system with me. I can only imagine how I would've dealt with postpartum if my mom didn't live here, if I didn't have my sister, and if my job forced me back to work weeks after giving birth to my child. I know I'm really lucky and blessed to have had their support.

When my mom had a kid back home, she would put on huruud and pamper herself. She did not understand why I was trying to lose the baby weight after my son's birth and discreetly tried to fatten me up. "Lose weight? You should enjoy it!"

She complained that my siblings and I didn't understand how to take care of ourselves. In the States, we were expected to rush back to work and erase any sign of pregnancy from our appearances as quickly as possible. This was unconscionable to my mother. For her, the months after childbirth were a joyous time filled with relaxation and self-care.

～

Minnesota is home. It's the home we made for ourselves. But I'm also afraid for my child in two ways. I am afraid he will get lost. Lost in the legal system and have his life thrown away. And I'm afraid he will get lost in the country and forget who he is. I will instill in him family values, like my parents and culture taught us. And we'll leave behind things like qabil and the idea of limits. When we were growing up, my parents always reminded us that we weren't American. As if we were guests in someone's home. I'm gonna raise my son to refuse to be a guest.

I am Somali, not "Somali American." I refuse to qualify my identity. Chinese and Black Americans have been here for hundreds of years, but they have to hyphenate or qualify their identities. This teaches us that to be American means to be White. Scandinavians and Germans who live in Minnesota never modify their identities; they are simply *American*. So why should we modify ours? Why should everyone besides White people qualify their American identity?

Assimilation and integration are fancy ways of saying "erase yourself." Most Americans never leave the United States, so they don't know how rich and vibrant other cultures are. Anyone who feels the need to assimilate doesn't understand what they're giving up in order to fit in.

I grew up with the melting pot analogy and eventually the salad bowl. To me, assimilating is like taking a beautiful filet mignon and mushing it up to ground beef in order to make meat loaf. Yes, technically it's still there, but was it worth it? The filet was more valuable as itself, before being churned through this machine.

There are parts of American culture I admire. I like the frankness and straightforwardness. We Somalis will dance around a subject for hours before getting to the point. My mom always used to say, "Americans will tell you their whole life," except who they voted for and how much money they make. What I love about Somali culture is our kinship. We care deeply about anything that relates to our people. I know if I went to Alaska today and saw a Somali person, the first thing they'd say is "Soomaali miya tahay?"

This is a beautiful thing, and it can also be a double-edged sword. We hold people to a different standard if they are Somali, like Congresswoman Ilhan Omar. There are things she's done that observers would allow anyone else to get away with, but because she is Somali they criticize her. A lot of gripes people have against her could easily be made about other candidates. People also have high expectations of her because she's a woman. It's one thing to have a political disagreement with her, but it's another entirely to have vitriol against her because of her personal decisions. We don't hold men to that same standard—and certainly not White people.

∽

For Somali people: Stop focusing on negatives; let's focus on the positives.

For Somali women and girls: As a people, we have come this far only because of Somali women and girls. Give yourselves credit. Take a day off from saving the rest of us. You deserve it. Here in Minnesota, Somali women reign supreme. Somali women run businesses, accomplish educational feats, and are breaking down doors in all professions. As a community, let's give credit where it's due.

For Somali men: It's important that you understand your role as fathers, brothers, and sons. You have an important role to play in modeling for the next generation what a man looks like. Don't let yourselves off the hook.

8

Qorsho Hassan, 30s, Louisiana

I was born in New Orleans, Louisiana. I was named after my dad's mother. My mom never liked the name because she felt it was too harsh, so I was alternatively called Hibaq. I came to love both of my names for different reasons. Hibaq was easy to love, but Qorsho took time. I love Qorsho now because of its fullness and richness, as well as the connection to my father and his family. And it's a hard name to forget because it demands to be acknowledged.

My mom and dad both came to the States in the eighties. My mother came to the States by herself on a visa to pursue a bachelor's in accounting. She's a very smart woman with a knack for mathematics. She met my father, a handyman with dreams of owning his own business. He helped get her brother sponsorship to come to America. That's when he fell in love with her and proposed. She was living in Virginia at the time, and he convinced her to move to Louisiana.

My sister Hoda and I were born in New Orleans. My birth was hard for my mother. It was a traumatic time for her and her family back home. I was coming into the world when she was dealing with strife in all areas of her life. Back home the Civil War was beginning and her family was struggling. It was a period of uncertainty and stress. My parents both left Somalia during a time of peace without knowing what was to come for their families who stayed.

My parents divorced. My mom tried her best to make a home out of New Orleans, but try as she might, it was never a fit, in more ways than one. My mom moved my sister and me to Toronto on a search for a better life. My dad remarried and went on to have more kids. When I was three years old, my father passed in a car accident back in the States. I always pray for my father. Every night before I go to sleep, I pray that his sins are absolved and his good deeds are accepted.

During this time in Toronto, my mother was working two jobs at a time. She was rarely home, and so my sister was my caretaker. She made a tremendous difference in my life. She taught me to read before I entered school, fed and bathed me, and even had the period talk. My sister Hoda was my role model, best friend, and protector from bullies. Everyone played their part. There was always this acknowledgment in our home that my mom, sister, and I survived this world and all it threw at us together. We had each other's backs, and it has helped make us closer.

My mom had very high expectations for us. She had us memorize times tables before I could even read. She stressed that we were to be excellent in all avenues of our lives as good students, good cooks, and good at keeping our homes. She was determined to make sure we knew how to take care of ourselves.

Our relationship was very strong when I was child. As a woman, my respect for her has only grown exponentially. She was my mom and dad. She took on that role. My sister and I are fighters because my mom was that. She moved us around so much because she was on a search for the best thing for her daughters. We moved fifteen times when I was a kid. We lived all over, from New Orleans to Toronto, Ottawa, Atlanta, Ohio, and now Minnesota. That's one thing I would change about our upbringing. Those seismic changes can impact a child greatly in ways they don't fully understand. Stability and routine are tremendously important to a person's sense of the world. If the world is always changing, how can you plan for it?

~

I'm so grateful to know who my grandparents were. The only grandparent I didn't meet was my mother's father. He was a general in the army. I still search for Awoowe Farax's photographs online in hopes that I may find him. I am my family's historian, and I have a chest of photos of my family. I love having something to remember my family by. From time to time, I compare photos of my dad to photos of his dad. My paternal grandfather was a very tall and distinct man. He visited us occasionally when we lived in Atlanta. He was a religious man, more religious than my dad. When he would see my dad, he would remind him to raise us with strong ties to our diin.

I'll never forget the will and mercy of Allah (سبحانه وتعالى). My sisters and I took a trip to London when I was in my early twenties to meet my father's side of the family. Before then, I had never met Ayeeyo Qorsho, my namesake, and if we had talked on the phone growing up, I was too young to remember. I'll never forget the first thing my grandmother said when she saw me: "Oh, he lives still." It still brings tears to my eyes to remember her words and love. As a child, I knew I looked very much like my dad and that we shared a temperament. This worried me, because I feared I would be just like my dad in other ways. My grandmother made me feel proud to be my father's daughter. I still hold on to that feeling and the memories she gave me of my father who I didn't have a chance to get to know. She gave me a link to him and brought his image to life. My grandmother never tired of sharing everything she loved about her favorite son.

That reunion was bittersweet, filled with tales of my dad and family, joy, and some natural resentment as well. We spent a month building relationships that we still have to this day and are very grateful to have made. One month later, Ayeeyo Qorsho was diagnosed with leukemia and passed away shortly after. I am still in awe of God's timing. I am grateful that I got to meet my grandmother and for the blessings she shared with us.

My maternal grandmother, Ayeeyo Asli, has continuously been a part of my life. When she came to the States, she lived with my mom and us. Just like with Ayeeyo Qorsho, her arrival had come not a moment too soon. She landed in Ohio, where we lived, a week before 9/11. Ayeeyo Asli had never met us and hadn't seen her own daughter in over ten years. She wanted to help raise us, and she stayed with us for over a year and a half. She had a profound effect on us in that short period of time. She injected gabay, baranbuur, and deep appreciation of Somali heritage into us. At a time when it was uncool and dangerous to be visibly Muslim, she taught us to be proud of our hijab and Islam. Even though we knew how to pray, she taught us how to pray intentionally and our purpose in prayer. She became our disciplinarian. Our mom never hit us and was very gentle with us growing up; she didn't even like to raise her voice. My ayeeyo was a spitfire woman with a zero-tolerance policy. She corrected our teenage sass and occasional disrespect.

Ayeeyo gave us structure and routine, which our mother couldn't offer because of her role as a full-time provider. Even though ayeeyo never actually whipped us, she whipped us into shape. She was there for a short time, but she had a lasting impact. She came to us during a time when peer pressure was very high and we were getting messages from all parts of our lives to conform and not stand out. "You're too Black, too Somali, too Muslim, too different." Here she was, a traditional Somali grandmother trying to instill this appreciation of diin and dhaqan into her very much Somali American grandkids. We learned from our grandmother to be straightforward and honest, qualities that my sister and I embody in adult life.

～

My education was very polarizing. We eventually moved to Atlanta, where I had some distinct memories of school. We went to an inner-city school. I was in ELL for a while and was constantly pulled out of class. I had a hard time connecting with my White teachers and did not receive much in the way of help from them. One time, I needed to use the bathroom really bad and, because I didn't speak English, I raised my hand and signaled my teacher, pointing to my privates to tell her that I needed to be excused. She ignored me, and I peed myself. It's the perfect metaphor for my education those first few years. I asked for help and was ignored.

I fit in with my peers because it was a predominantly Black and Brown student body. I was learning a lot more than most students at this stage. I was learning not just our studies, but also English and American customs. I remember I was very comfortable eating with my hands during meals, but for my peers that wasn't a normal thing to do. It was not unusual to see me chowing down on grits, turkey sausage, and eggs with my hands. Grits was really just soor, right? And at home, we eat soor with our hands. I spent time really learning and unlearning my own culture and learning American culture.

For a long time, I was the bad kid. I was not doing well in school. I didn't understand the rules, and sometimes I didn't want to understand the rules. I remember having my own island to keep me separate from the rest of the students. I didn't connect well with teachers, who saw me as a bad kid or a kid who couldn't learn grade level, so why try with her? In fourth grade, I had Ms. Fulmer. The first time I saw her I said, "You're not Hoda's fourth-grade teacher, so you're not my teacher!" She took that as a challenge to crack me. I now have the same rapport with my own students who might struggle in the classroom.

She got to know me. She helped me fall in love with reading. She saw me as an emerging reader, not a struggling reader, which I appreciate now as a teacher—it wasn't deficit based. She wanted to know about my culture and my favorite Somali singers. I would sing her Saado Cali songs, and she made me feel seen in the classroom. My grades turned around and I thrived at school. For the first time, I was meeting marks in state assessments. I graduated from the ELL program. I had a strong academic year, which set the tone for the rest of my education and eventually my career.

My mom took my academic excellence as a sign that we were not being challenged. During this time, rent prices were going up, and we did not have access to housing support that would allow us to afford living there. We moved to Ohio, where I finished the rest of my education. I started fifth grade in Hilliard and experienced a culture shock. In Atlanta I was one of many; here I was one of few. I was the only Black kid in some of my classes and the only hijabi in most. I stuck out like a sore thumb. As much as I tried to blend in, I was hyper-visible. Every time the topic of race or Muslims or anything non-White came up, all eyes were glued to me, and that included the teacher. I was an unwilling spokesperson for all people of color. Here I witnessed the difference in resources and quality compared to the bare minimum support we got in Atlanta. I started to understand that this was how racism played out. In Atlanta, I didn't know I was Black because I was surrounded by Blackness. It wasn't something apparent. I didn't think I had limitations because of my Blackness, and I didn't internalize an inferiority complex. In Ohio, I realized not only that being Black was important, but that it was seen as a deficit by my peers and teachers.

My mom gave us no option but to go to college. It wasn't a question. In a way, we were making up for the education she had to quit in order to raise us. Thankfully, I could follow my sister's footsteps in my journey to college, because no one else could prepare us for FAFSA and scholarships. My sister went out of state, and I got a full ride to Ohio State. College was very different from my K–12 experience. I followed in my sister's footsteps again and went into premed. I had a depressive state in sophomore year and realized that premed wasn't for me. I could study whatever I wanted and had ownership over my education. I dived into social sciences, learning about a different history than the whitewashed one from my suburban school. It was at once exhilarating and terrifying, having this much choice. I found teachers and networks I connected with and people who empowered me.

I studied abroad my junior year and went to Poland for a semester. I had never lived away from my family, but I wanted to experience something new. I studied the Tatar community, a group of Muslim Poles and a minority in Poland. I also studied the tolerance level of non-Muslim Polish people toward them. I ate perogies and had White people stare at me in confusion, probably wondering why this Black Somali Muslim American was in their country. But it was a freeing moment. Here I am, a Somali woman, doing my thing in Poland. Who would've thought? And I came back with even more purpose and confidence. I felt like my own person.

I did AmeriCorps my senior year, and that experience pushed me deeper into teaching. I won a Fulbright Fellowship to teach in Malaysia and packed my bags. I taught at a school that was 60 percent Malay students. The school had a large male population but a diverse student body of Malays, Chinese, and Indians. For context, 68 percent of Malaysia's population is ethnic Malays. I was afraid I wouldn't be able to connect with the students or they wouldn't understand me. There were tensions in the school because of the mixture in demographics. I had Malay, Chinese, and Indian students. The Chinese and Indian students faced racism and discrimination. As a Muslim, I didn't want them to think I would automatically be against them and side with the Malay kids. Malay schools place all the struggling students in one class. It's the class other teachers dread getting because of the difficulty in teaching. On the first day of lessons, I asked the students how to say common phrases in their native languages. This shocked them. They couldn't believe that I was interested in learning about them and their cultures. They were shocked that I gave them the same attention as, if not more than, the Malay students. That set a tone of equity in the classroom. They were suspicious before—they had a right to be—but now they knew they could trust me. After that day, they embraced me as their teacher and the students had a blast. It was my favorite class to teach.

That year in Malaysia was truly a learning experience, in more ways than one. I had to learn how to advocate for myself and navigate a country that is not necessarily built for independent women. I traveled with friends and experienced the world. I knew then that I could do anything. My fears of being away from my home and family melted away. I came back to Ohio with a newfound confidence and determination.

When I settled back in Ohio, I went through a culture shock. I had spent a year acclimating myself to life in Malaysia, and I had forgotten what it was like to live in the States. I had to transition to life in Columbus. I fought the pull to be a teacher. I went through a period of uncertainty. Eventually, I started teaching at an inner-city charter school in the Columbus area that predominantly served Somali students and other people of color. And once that opportunity fell in my lap, I thought, *this is meant to be*. I started doing community work in the area where I lived. This had a really profound effect on me and taught me what community work should look like. With a friend, Ruth Smith, I interviewed Somali youth about their experiences and wrote a book titled *Urur Dhex-Dhexaad Ah: Community In-Between*. We created and held an exhibit at the Dublin Arts Council in Ohio that supported the contributions of young Somalis, highlighting their work and giving nuance to a single story. We wanted to see authentic stories that weren't molded by White consumption of the immigrant narrative. I really began building a home and legacy around me.

That project became my goodbye. It was closure with a place that I loved, that I found myself in, that I struggle with, that I became a woman in.

The goodbye came in the form of my sister's match day, the day she learned where she would have her residency. My sister had matched with a Twin Cities hospital. Because we are a family, we wouldn't let Hoda pursue this alone. We had a big decision to make. My sister told me, "Well actually, Qorsho, you have a big decision to make, since you're the one who prays istikhara more than us." I prayed often. This was a terrifying realization, that I held the power to at once say goodbye to my home and welcome my sister's future. I asked Allah (سبحانه وتعالى) fervently, "Is there a benefit or purpose in us moving to Minnesota?" And I felt a peace after. That was how we made the decision. I finished up my last year at the charter school, and we packed our bags and moved to Minnesota.

∽

The first year we lived in Minnesota, I flew back to Ohio four times. I really wanted to hate Minnesota. I had it set in my mind that I wouldn't like it. There are many things I don't like. I don't like incessant small talk. I often find myself in conversations about the weather, fruit salad, and pies. This common habit seems so extraneous. But I realized after a while that White peers will sometimes engage with me just to appear progressive to other White people. They will also behave one way toward me but talk about me in a different way or act differently toward other people. Because I am a Black woman, people love to tokenize me and my work, but when I disagree or speak up, I am labeled combative or violent. White people here are really two-faced. In Ohio, racism was very overt. It was horrible, but at least everyone knew where they stood. Here, it's hidden under the surface like a riptide, and just as dangerous. "You don't value my humanity but you're smiling in my face."

But in many ways I came to love Minnesota. I love the summer; I could do without the winter. Love praying in the beautiful Minnesota nature and being in tune with Allah (سبحانه وتعالى) and His creations.

I especially love the community in Minnesota. I see a lot of selflessness and holistic organizing that leaves agency to the people. These are the things I find endearing about Minnesota.

In my year of transition, I was very selective about where I wanted to teach next. I picked the Burnsville area schools because I think it's really important as a Black educator to be intentional about whom I serve and how I serve. I am a teacher at a Burnsville elementary school in a school district that has a large Black and Brown student body, in particular Somali students. My students bring me great joy, and I thoroughly enjoy being in the classroom. Black educators can relate to this experience of students naturally gravitating toward us. Students sense we can relate to them and want to get to know us the same way we want to get to know them. It's very rewarding.

If you'd have told me in 2019 that I would be named Minnesota Teacher of the Year in 2020, I would've laughed. I'm still in awe, for a couple reasons. This is my ninth year of teaching, but I didn't know that my work was that impactful or being seen as that impactful. When I was named, I remember being overwhelmed. I'm a private person, and I struggle with attention—and this was a recognition that would demand attention and even bring backlash. Was I willing to welcome that? On the other hand, I knew how huge this moment would be, not just for me and my family but for all Somalis everywhere. I knew this would reach the diaspora, wherever they were, and our people back home. I was grateful for my mom's upbringing as a giver, because it helped me recognize the title wasn't just for me but that I was breaking down a wall. I was amplifying my students' and my community's needs and voices.

The community made sure I felt the love. The news of my award is still reaching different parts of the world. I even saw Minnesota Somalis and Ohio Somalis playfully fighting over who gets to claim me and the award. I was able to give interviews in the Somali language to make sure this was accessible to Somalis in Somalia, not just those who spoke English. One moment that stands out is when the Somali community held a celebration at the Brian Coyle Center in the Cedar-Riverside neighborhood, a historic Somali neighborhood in Minneapolis. The love my family and I received was monumental.

I shared this moment with my mother in particular. It brings tears to my eyes because she never got her chance to shine, and my story is truly her story. She's been by my side the whole time, and every opportunity I have to speak, she gets to share her wisdom and way of parenting with the world. We jokingly call her a public speaker. She was nervous at first, but we encouraged her. After all, she is the mother of the 2020 Minnesota Teacher of the Year. She has to tell her story, because I surely did not get here by myself! It's nice to celebrate this moment with my White peers as educators in America. But it's so special to share this moment with my community.

⁓

COVID-19 fundamentally changed the country and the world. We experienced the horror at home, worried about Ayeeyo Asli's health during this pandemic. We feared hearing about her death over the phone, as my mother had experienced so many deaths back home. I remember my first memory of transnational grief was watching my mother go in her closet and cry after hearing about news back home, hiding so that we would not see her that way. I did not want my mom to experience her own mother's death in this way.

We experienced horror in the classroom as schools were shut down. Seemingly overnight, we were to convert our homes into classrooms. I did not have the same space as my White peers and could not convert a guest room or the den into a classroom. I had to convert my own bedroom into a class for my students. If I had terrible work-life balance before, quarantine has destroyed it. I sleep four to five hours a night on average and spend most of my time prepping for class or teaching it. I also worry deeply about my students who are not transitioning well. They already have a lot to deal with at home, and the new distance learning has only added to their barriers. My experience is not unlike many other teachers trying to make the unworkable work for the sake of our kids.

This summer, we experienced the murder of George Floyd. His death launched worldwide protests starting right here at home. Floyd's death reminded me of my first experience with a cop in Minnesota. I was driving home during Ramadan with my mom. The time to break our fasts had passed, and I was impatient to get home and get to a meal. In my impatience, I crossed a long white line in order to merge onto the highway instead of waiting for the line to become dotted. Immediately, I saw the red and blue lights of a cop and heard sirens. I'm already an anxious driver because of the way my father passed away. I pulled over, anxious, having never been pulled over before. My heart was pounding in my chest, and my mom was reading Surah Fatiha. I remember thinking, *Why am I so afraid for my life right now? What have I done to be afraid to die?* The officer knocked on my window and asked in a slow, exaggerated way if I knew why I was being pulled over. He was condescending, and it set the tone for the rest of the encounter. I had experienced microaggressions. I had experienced racism before. But this particular moment really stuck out to me. I thought to myself, *this is Minnesota nice: this man is smiling at me and has his hand on his holster at the same time.* He could shoot and kill me and still be smiling, in the same second. This was a jarring juxtaposition that only further emphasized the polite and deadly racism of the North. He questioned why I had Ohio insurance, and this encouraged his assumption that I was not from here and did not know any rules. He started rattling off all the violations he saw in my car, that my music (my Qur'an) was too loud, I shouldn't have prayer beads on my rearview mirror, and so on and so forth. I was getting frustrated: how did crossing a white line turn into this? That simple traffic stop took one whole hour to finish. It felt like the longest sixty minutes of my life. After he left, I remember crying with my mother all the way home.

Back in Ohio, we had seen police brutality. Like the murder of fourteen-year-old Tamir Rice for playing with a toy gun at a playground. But experiencing it in real life was so jarring. And George Floyd's death made me go back to that place in my mind. I buried that experience, not wanting to talk about it even to my sisters. But to hear George Floyd calling out for his mother broke my heart. Because I imagined if I had a few words left in me before I was dying, I would also cry out for Hooyo.

Being a teacher, I had always made it a point to teach my students about loving themselves, being proud of their ethnicity, their culture. Having a discussion with my kids about George Floyd and Black lives, not in person but virtually, was very hard. It was hard for me as a Black person to share my Black and Brown students' grief and their processing. But I knew that I needed to create that space for them. And I knew that my White students needed to listen very closely. It wasn't a time for them to share but to listen, learn, be better, and change. I felt this responsibility as a teacher to interrupt White supremacy. Even the police officers who killed George Floyd had probably attended a school such as the one I taught at. Were they ever engaged about racism and taught by teachers to view others with empathy?

I felt like I was living in two pandemics, COVID-19 and the protests. I couldn't just sit at home while the people were calling for justice. My mom was afraid for me. I asked her why; I had protested before. But my mom said this felt like a powder keg, that things were different. And even though our lives were at risk, I felt protected by my fellow protestors. Whenever my friends and I needed to pray, protesters lined a protective circle around us. I was also protesting because I know Saado Cali, the great fanaan, would be here if she were alive. She criticized the Somali government gracefully and tactfully through song. I saw so many Somali women of all ages protesting and being in community with their African American brothers and sisters. I wanted to preserve that moment of unity, because we came together not just in our grief and anger but also in joy.

Given the climate after George Floyd's murder and the uprising, I knew students needed space to process their emotions, ask questions, and think critically about their community. Our conversations in the beginning of the 2020–21 school year were centered around identity, community building, and inclusivity.

Students brought up experiences with racism, but we didn't discuss George Floyd or the uprising. I waited until later in the semester to talk about police brutality because I didn't want to start off the school year with more trauma for my Black students. They needed their learning space to be loving and affirming first. When we finally talked about George Floyd, I was wrapping up the community unit with a picture book called *Something Happened in Our Town*. It's a story about racial injustices that occur in a town, in which the story stirs up a conversation between a White family and an African American family. It explains how they process the death of an unarmed Black man at the hands of police. The students processed their experiences with race and racism. It was a really powerful conversation that went beyond just being "nice" or "kind." It's about being intentionally anti-racist and anti-xenophobic and not just interrupting racism but disrupting it. I think some adults want to shield children from these conversations or think they aren't ready to have these conversations. But kids are very much in tune with the world around them because of social media and the digital age. My students were able to have really deep and meaningful conversations about race and racism. I knew they were prepared, but I was really proud of them for leaning in.

The family of one of my students did not like the content of the book. Instead of stating their concerns directly to me or school leaders, they shared their concerns with an influential police officer in the Bloomington area. This officer then made a public Facebook post about the book and my classroom. This further garnered the attention of the largest police association of Minnesota. They released a statement, calling out the governor—who had recommended the book—the Minnesota Department of Education, and the Minnesota Department of Health, as well as calling out my school and my grade level. This was a deliberate attempt to censor my classroom and the literature we read. But also a deliberate attempt to stop the conversations teachers are having with students about the police state and state-sanctioned violence. The police union was intentional about not using my name but made sure to give enough identifying information that a simple Google search would bring up my name and title. I have dealt with being escorted out of my school building due to a safety threat, misinformation, and countless harmful and violent messages and comments and have been called out by alt-right media. Their message is to "send her back" and "zero tolerance to teachers who use books like this."

This was an act of intimidation.

My school leaders, in particular my White school leader, were very dismissive about this at first, which says a lot about his White male privilege. There was a lack of empathy and awareness of what had even happened. His first statement to me was, "A police officer has posted about you on Facebook." He couldn't imagine, in the midst of worldwide protests at George Floyd's murder, how triggering this could be, given my experiences as a Black woman and my experience with police. That initial conversation set a tone in my school district in which they did not want to address this. When I received media requests or press left and right, they told me not to respond out of concern for my safety. They made it seem like they were looking out for me, but in reality they were looking out for their image. They did not want to support anti-racist teaching and/or this book, and therefore did not want to support me.

The school district had no problem tokenizing my identity and title for their image. I appear on their website, YouTube page, and social media. I'm highlighted as a teacher they are proud of. But they are not proud of what I have to say and what I believe in. My message is that my platform is to amplify marginalized voices. And they've literally silenced me for doing so. Their silence is complicit and racist. My school leaders have taken a stance in which they don't want to push back on the district because they're afraid of the backlash they might receive. Not realizing that I have already received the backlash, in immense proportion. And I carry that weight along with that of being a Black educator, a Black female educator who already carries a lot of weight on her shoulders. The school has demonstrated that they will uplift and share in my honor and accolades, but only when it benefits them. This was an opportunity to show students we stand with them, and it was squandered out of cowardice when the time called for courage.

When I heard about the Facebook post, my first reaction wasn't fear but anger. I was upset at how these opponents portrayed me and my teaching. I was angry at the power they had and felt vindicated that the little bit of power I took from them elicited this response in the police union. They were exposing their own fragile egos and going after a fourth-grade teacher. They expected me to back down and go quietly, be embarrassed about creating a conversation on racism and police in my classroom. They did not expect me to buck back. The irony of it all is that I was not the only teacher reading this book. Several White teachers were reading it to students too. But it was me who was singled out by the police union and silenced by the district. When White teachers teach anti-racism, they are praised and recognized. When a Black teacher teaches anti-racism, that is seen as a threat and dangerous. Is it because people hate the message or is it because it suddenly becomes dangerous when a Black Somali Muslim woman says it?

The interesting thing about allies is that they say all the right things in front of you. They are actively anti-racist when they're around the right group of people. But when they aren't, and they are in a moment requiring moral courage, they move back into their own safety and continue as is. They follow the status quo. I felt this intensely. At my school, we have a few teachers of color and I am one of five Black teachers. When the story broke, there was an immense outpouring of White teachers coming to me to console me and tell me they've got my back. They asked, "What do you need? How can I support you?" They saw me as this savior who was going to point to the solution, fix the problem, and make everyone feel good—all before lunch. Instead I asked, "What have you been doing?" and "Why haven't you taken action so far?" Racism at this school existed long before this one situation, so why was it something we could ignore until a teacher was publicly affected? Some backed down and went back to apathy. Others took it to heart and are now standing in front of me, not just behind me. Teachers, whether we like it or not, are a part of a system that devalues Black and Brown lives. We can be complicit and ignore it, or we can fight to create a world worthy of our students. If you're not actively anti-racist, then being a teacher is not for you. Students need more from their teachers than passive nonracists. Fight for your students, or get out of the way for those of us who will.

I hid the situation from my family, in particular my mother. For one, I'm a Somali woman. I saw my mom bottle things up and carry on, and it's something I instinctively do. Even when I received the Teacher of the Year award, there were so many racist and vile comments all over social media from people who hated to see a Black Somali Muslim win the award. I internalized it and moved on as much as I could. I also didn't want my mom to worry about me any more than she already does. My family didn't ask for this attention or exposure; it was something I subjected them to. I didn't ask for it either, but it was for me to deal with. When I told Hooyo, her first words to me were, "Illahi baa ka weyn." God is bigger than this. God is bigger than them.

Because of the backlash, this could potentially jeopardize my nomination and standing to be awarded National Teacher of the Year. Here's the truth of the matter. I was the same Black educator before the Minnesota award and before the backlash. If I'm not awarded the title for that reason—because of the racist backlash—then it's not something I want. Why would I want a title that's going to silence me? Why would I want a title that would have me teach differently? Or interact with my students differently? Or not call out the system for what it is? I will not change my anti-racist beliefs and teachings in order to be recognized or gain approval. I will not change myself.

Before this situation, I hadn't questioned being an educator. But the truth is that this year has inextricably changed me. If I wasn't tired before, I am exhausted now. I've been giving and pouring into others so much, I'm not sure how much more I can take. I haven't gotten a break, a chance to breathe or even digest what's happened this year. It's been one thing after another that has called for my attention and effort. Self-care is a luxury that Black people can't always afford. We give and give and give until we can't. As Black educators, we're stuck in the cycle of racism. The irony that I caught a racist backlash for teaching students about racism is not lost on me. My students give me hope with how they see the world. They are problem solvers and investigators and a lot smarter than adults give them credit for. They want to work through problems and are courageous. As cheesy as it sounds, I feel like our future is in good hands.

～

I cope through faith. Women in my life taught me to remember of God in times of happiness and in times of sorrow. When I won the award, the first word I uttered was "Alhamdulilah." My faith was instilled in me at an early age. I listened to Qur'an through cassette tapes, Mom taught us our duas, I slept every night having made dua for my family but especially my late dad. Growing up, I went to dugsi. We focused on memorization, but I wish we learned a variety of things. I'm reminded that I am most grateful to be a Muslim. I'm comforted by this verse: "O you who have believed seek help in patience and prayer surely Allah is with the patient" (Qur'an 2:153). I find comfort in that and remind myself to be patient and trusting of Allah (سبحانه وتعالى).

I identify as a Black Somali American. My culture and faith are a strong part of my identity. Growing up in the States, I have seen a cultural gap between generations. Some of this stems from young people trying to make a way and leave certain parts of the culture, like tribalism, behind. It worries older generations because it feels like a rejection of the whole culture, but it's not. Just like they made their own way, it's now time to offer young people the same grace. Language and communication is a barrier as well, and it goes both directions. Young people are losing Somali as they access it less and less. They are mocked for not speaking it well and painted as less Somali or arrogant for somehow forgetting their native tongue. Language is not the only indicator of culture—there are so many other facets. Some older people abstain from learning English and take pride in doing so. The problem becomes that these two generations cannot communicate with each other, and we are essentially cut off from each other. We have to find ways to communicate because otherwise we risk further alienating ourselves from each other. We should be finding common ground, not pointing and blaming.

Assimilation is a pathway to cultural genocide. Intentional integration or acculturation is okay: we should be learning from each other. Our differences are not a disadvantage; they are an advantage.

⤳

To Somalis: we are brilliant and capable. We are a beautiful group of people who are also individuals and are even stronger as a collective. We support and uplift each other in our victories, but sometimes we struggle with being reflective in our shortcomings and failures. Those shortcomings are also a part of our story. I hope as a people we can rebuild an even stronger home so that we are not forever searching for one, insh'Allah.

To Somali girls and women: our powerful intersectionalities—being women, being Black, being Somali—are sometimes seen as barriers, but they make us stronger. Those identities will help you experience rich moments in your life, when you connect with others in a unique, immeasurable way. When you're in community or even one-on-one with your sisters, you will share that bond. Let's insist that we find ways to be together, so that we may find healing and a way forward. We deserve to have those experiences and to have that be just for us.

To Somali boys and men: so many aspects of our culture are passed down maternally, and Somali people have such an admirable high regard for mothers. It shows in the phrase "Home is where Hooyo is." I see the respect Somali men have for their mothers, but I don't see that transferred to their female peers. I worry about that disconnect because it creates opportunities for Somali women to be harmed and silenced—such as policing the way a woman chooses to wear hijab and inserting oneself into that personal journey. If Somali men reflected on why they should respect not just Somali mothers but all Somali women and honor them and give them space to be themselves, then Somali men would be elevated and increase their regard. I want my nephew Sulayman to one day actively work against systems of misogyny. To not just say stop or be a bystander, but to be a man who does not allow harm against women to happen in his presence. I have that same high expectation for my Somali brothers and want them to do better. If you can do that, you will be a force to be reckoned with, like Somali women.

9

Roun Said, 30s, Atlanta, Georgia

My name is an old-school, authentic Somali name. I don't know what it means, perhaps a general goodness. I just know it's not common. I was named by my dad after his older sister. I am the oldest of seven kids.

I was born and raised in Atlanta, Georgia. A lot of the Somalis in Atlanta came in the seventies or early eighties on student visas or were sponsored. A good number came after the war of '77. Many of them came from middle-class backgrounds. My dad was sponsored by a White man in Florida. This man sponsored my dad and a bunch of other guys to come to the States. I think the man was perhaps a humanitarian or just an altruistic person; I never heard the full story. The guys and my dad stayed with the man briefly in Florida before coming to Atlanta. They created a beautiful well-knit community in Atlanta. Even though they came from different places back in Somalia and different stations in life, they forged a life together in this new country. This community in Atlanta is different from others. I appreciated the uniqueness of the community in Atlanta.

Mom came to America in '87 and had me shortly after. When Mom gave birth to me she did not speak English, so I'm blown away with how she navigated the health care systems. She didn't have any family here in the country at that time. She also wasn't able to directly call them, so they communicated through letters. They sent letters to Ethiopia because that's where their families are from. Dad grew up near Jigjiga and later in Hargeisa. Mom was born in Addis Ababa and briefly grew up in Jigjiga and moved to Hargeisa. My dad sent for my mom after he came to the States. They had met and married back home before my mom made the journey.

My dad has worked all sorts of jobs. He used to be a waiter, then a taxi driver, and then he worked at a warehouse. Now he is a truck driver. He's done that for the past ten or fifteen years. We moved to Ohio after Atlanta. Then we moved to Maine for a short time. Lewiston was an interesting town. There were a lot of new arrivals and a Bantu Somali community. I learned about the discrimination Bantu Somalis face, and the way some have fought to be recognized independently of the Somali community. Others call it divisive, but I remember speaking with a woman who told me that by not having their own designation, it's as if they're ignoring their history and being lumped in with people who don't accept them. Maine is where I witnessed the diversity in our community but also how the pain that occurred back home is brought here and is ongoing and alive. We eventually moved back to Ohio because Maine didn't have as many opportunities for higher education.

We lived in Columbus, Ohio, for many years. Columbus has a growing Somali community. We knew Somalis from all over. The community was very close. The people in Ohio were very business minded, and I saw Somalis opening up shops, law offices, and different types of organizations and small businesses. I attended Ohio State and began working as a mental health therapist.

∿

I moved to Minnesota with my husband a couple of years ago. My husband is an engineer, and he was supposed to travel a lot in Minnesota and Iowa. We thought it made sense to keep us close. I also wanted to do therapy work with Somalis and felt there was better opportunity in Minnesota. Minneapolis has a lot of energy and is very active. Minnesota attracted us because we also wanted better education and Islamic education for our three kids. Ultimately, there was a chance for a better life in Minneapolis, and we took a leap of faith. We lived in Shakopee for some time but moved to Minneapolis for a shorter commute.

My kids were enrolled in predominantly White schools in the suburbs, and I wanted them to have a different experience than I did. I wanted to protect them from feeling out of place and being treated like tokens. I wanted them to have a diverse educational experience, so we took them to a different school district.

In Atlanta, I grew up in a predominantly Black area. I went to an inner-city school with students and some staff who looked like me. Even our curriculum had a Black empowerment element. We learned about historical Black figures, movements, and leaders. There was also a personal development component: we were taught that we can accomplish anything we set our minds to. Our race wasn't treated as something that was a detriment or barrier, but instead this idea of greatness was intentionally reinforced and supported. It was only when we moved to a Whiter area that my race began to stand out to me in a different way. I became one of the few Black students in my classes. And as I progressed further in my education, it just got Whiter and Whiter. It was so different from the way I grew up in a Black home in a Black neighborhood with Black kids. I was used to being similar to my peers. Having to go from being one of many to one of few was jarring. Coupled with becoming the spokesperson for an entire race, this feeling of being different and standing out didn't sit well with me. People were also surprised by the achievement and academic success of Black students. They made assumptions not only about who we were but about what we were capable of. I came from a diverse group of people, and it didn't make sense to minimize us down to one immutable trait. But I came to understand that's how some people view us.

I'm an American. I was born in this country. It's the only place I've ever known as home, the place I'm connected to. When I was a kid, that was so straightforward to me. What else could it mean? But growing up, and because of the climate we live in, I've had to start asking myself, what does "being American" mean? I don't identify with the global perception of Americans. People think Americans are dumb because of the president we elected, or they say that we don't think for ourselves, and that certainly doesn't represent me. Before, I would be prouder to be American.

It was something I didn't even have to question or hesitate about. Growing up, I would say "I'm American" before I would say "I'm Somali" because I had no connection to Somalia. Sure, I spoke the language and my parents were Somali, but that was their experience. I had a different experience growing up in the States. Somalia was this foreign place to me, far removed from my own day-to-day life. But as I've gotten older, and having gone back home to visit, my perception has shifted. I call Somalia home when I talk about it. I'm no longer solely American; it's more nuanced for me.

In our generation, there's a push to go back home in order to help fix it. While the intentions are noble, I have to push back. Are we duplicating this idea of a White savior complex, where we think we can fix the problems of a people better than they can themselves? We don't necessarily know the landscape or political climate because we don't live there. Now we're swooping in to save the day, and we can unintentionally cause more damage. Can you imagine if a Somali from Finland came to Minneapolis to save us? We would laugh at him because of the arrogance it would show to come and fix our problems with his experiences and education. Instead, the question should be framed about how we can support the people already on the ground and work alongside them, not ahead of them. There are a lot of educated people back home. How can we elevate them? How can we support them? The other part of this is that we have a lot of work to do here in our own backyards. There are lots of people here who could utilize services and resources. We are here; we know our problems and are capable of rising to the occasion. It's a two-pronged approach that can help us do the most good and avoid the most harm. I know we're giving a great deal of support through remittances, and that should be recognized and applauded. But we need to be mindful and intentional about how we go about long-term support.

∽

I was close to my dad growing up, but I feel even closer to him now. We have a lot in common, like our love of reading. Our thing was to go to the library together. He would go to his section and I would go to mine, and we'd emerge arms overflowing with books to read.

Our parents experienced an initial loss back home, but it wasn't their only loss. There's also that secondary traumatization of hearing what your family members went through. Or getting those late-night phone calls of something happening. That impacts people tremendously. And I feel like that played a role in how connected my dad was as a parent. He was very hands-on. A very involved dad. But I know being the only one of his family here and hearing all the things that his family has gone through probably was a factor for him. And then I went through that stage as a teenager when you just don't want anything to do with your parents. And then after I had my own kids, it inspired me to foster that bond in our relationship. We never lost connection, but we were able to grow closer.

I've always been fascinated by my dad's stories. I wanted to hear the places he'd been, the stories he remembered, and the things he's experienced. And it doesn't always come out so easily. But little by little, I've been able to hear his stories. And a part of me is sad that I didn't start doing this when I was younger. I would've loved to learn about our culture through stories, about where we came from and his own experiences as a kid. I feel sad that I may have missed out on a lot of good stories that could've shaped me, helped me learn more about the world and myself. I think part of it is being that self-centered American kid. But another part is that I missed out on those stories because I didn't ask and I wasn't told. Alhamdulilah, we still are here together. It's a blessing to still have both my parents.

When I was on my journey to college, I did a lot of trial by error. I learned that by myself. Writing essays, applying for schools, college visits, applying for FAFSA, all on my own. So when it was my siblings' time to go that route, my parents were like, "Can you help them? Can you do this?" I became a part-time College Possible coach. I know immigrant kids can relate.

I was also dealing with institutions that my American friends didn't have to. I was reading letters from the Immigration and

Naturalization Service and writing emails addressed to different departments. When it came time to pick a college to attend, I was limited by how far I could be from my family. I needed to go somewhere close to home, whereas my peers were imagining life on campus. When I made life decisions, my sole objective wasn't just what I wanted. I had to consider the needs of my family.

~

My career trajectory wasn't straightforward, by any measure. I initially went to school to become a pediatric oncologist. I wanted to work with kids and help their families through tough times. After years of studies, I found it wasn't for me. I learned more about family social sciences. I knew, no matter what, I wanted to help people. I decided to go into therapy toward the end of my undergraduate studies. Then I went to graduate school for that degree and to get my license to practice therapy. But it's definitely not where I imagined myself to be.

I am a mental health therapist. This past year, I decided to go back to school for my PhD in family social science. I am in the first semester of my program. My research is about how trauma impacts parenting in Somali families. I'm also interested in exploring identity conflict in youth. Ideally, I see myself in an educator role and also doing research alongside my community. Perhaps in program development for education. This is a huge field to explore and an opportunity to make practical discoveries in the way of parenting and education. If I could do anything in the world, I would probably be a writer. I'd love to write a book about the lessons I've learned as a parent and navigating motherhood. I think one day I will.

~

I identify as Black. I used to say African American, but as I gain more awareness, I'm more hesitant to use it. I know we don't share the same history as African Americans. On an application, I check off Black or African American because Somali is a bit more nuanced identity. It's what I identify as ethnically for sure. I identify as Somali American. That best encapsulates my experience. It's been a journey of self-discovery. I started out with American. Then it was American Somali because I identified more with that American part of me. But now it's Somali American. I see it as a fifty-fifty divide. One part is who I am and the other is where I'm from.

I've come to recognize the privilege of my citizenship. I always took it for granted, just something I have. I was born American, and like most Americans, it's something I never had to think about. Knowing how hard it is to become a citizen and the hoops people have to go through—that's something that can't be ignored. In this country, undocumented migrants have been vilified by the person holding the highest office. They're treated like they're less than others, and people hold a low view of them. We see the rhetoric play out in policy, with families being separated and people being deported. Whereas before people were still being deported, now it's undeniable and up front. It's a travesty that people treat other human beings this way.

Some people who have long held animosity toward people different from themselves have been emboldened by Trump. That in itself is scary. The other part of the equation is the way Trump's rise has made us view others. For example, before Trump, I assumed others were okay with us. Now I'm more cautious in certain neighborhoods or the farther I get out of the city. Racists are pushing the envelope more and more, just to see what they can get away with. That's a terrifying thing to understand and raise a family in the midst of. How do you protect your family? How do you protect not only your kids' safety but also their sense of self?

As a mom and working academic, I'm not sure I've found the perfect balance yet. My load is dependent on the season, and it's often shifting. What it looks like right now may not be what it looks like next year. But one thing is for sure: I am very intentional about how I spend my time. It's easy to be so overwhelmed with responsibility that we become unfocused in our time. I used to be at work thinking about my kids, and then when I was with my kids I'd be thinking about some upcoming deadline. That's no way to live a life. We owe it to ourselves and those we love to be present. So when I'm with my kids, I'm not thinking about XYZ that needs to get done; I'm focused on my kids—and vice versa. I'm also very intentional about finding time for myself. Moms get really busy with taking care of their kids and their relationship with their partner. It's easy to lose sight of who we are outside of those titles and responsibilities. We lose touch with who we were before we were wives and moms. But it doesn't have to be a zero-sum game. I am who I am *and* I am a mom and wife. It's about enjoying our hobbies, spending time with ourselves, and keeping those parts alive in us. Yes, things change and so does life. But it's important to make time for yourself, not to lose sight of yourself. I'm the person who has to navigate my responsibilities, right? As moms, we have to make sure we don't get left behind.

I'm really blessed to have a village of mothers to lean on for support. I found my tribe of moms who come from all walks of life and are navigating motherhood together. Some of us are at home, others are working outside the home, and others are in school. We're all trying to figure it out. I'm learning to be more vocal about what I need because they're ready to step up for me. It's nice to know that we're not alone. We also share similar goals and parenting styles. We focus on positive parenting, being a safe space for our kids, and instilling an Islamic upbringing. Our parenting philosophy is a well-rounded one, where it's not just physical well-being that is taken care of but emotional well-being as well. There's a love language of physical support which is all the basic needs of food, clothing, shelter, and so on and so forth. But it's also really important to nurture the emotional needs of our kids.

We do have generational differences. One thing that comes to mind is how we've navigated being in the States. I'm navigating it as a person who was born here, whose first language is English, who understands the culture and the nuances. Our parents are navigating it as people who were not born here, who didn't speak the language, who had to learn and are probably still learning the culture and its nuances. And they raised kids in a culture that they don't fully understand, whereas I'm raising my kids in a culture that I do know how to navigate. Our parents had to learn alongside us.

Somali parents in my generation have stressors that look different from our parents'. We understand parenting to be a compromise of different aspects that are needed. We're generally more willing to make concessions and be flexible, depending on the needs of our families. Whereas our parents had more stressors. Not only were they worrying about family, they were also navigating a new culture while bringing their own culture with them. Naturally, they raised their kids the way they were raised, but the difference is that their kids are not living the way they lived. Not only are we in a different country and culture, we might have different stations in life or the resources available back home are not available here. Things are different in really profound ways and in simple ways. I think those are some of the differences that played a role.

~

Being the oldest in a Somali family is a lot of responsibility because you're made to be the example. You're the leader. Everyone's gonna follow you one day, so make sure you don't make any mistakes. And then, being the eldest daughter is an entirely other level. There's already a lot of responsibilities in a Somali family that come with being a daughter, much less the eldest. There's a lot that you're expected to do. You're constantly juggling roles. "I have to do the cooking and the cleaning and filling out forms for my parents and then go to this appointment with Mom—wait, did I remind so-and-so to get ready for school?" It doesn't stop when you grow up or start your own family. Even now, I get phone calls about navigating a situation. We fit into all these extra roles that other kids wouldn't necessarily have to do. It's a lot to take on, especially when you're figuring out the world for yourself and your family.

One thing I would have changed about how I was raised is tied to emotional connections. I would really have appreciated having more one-on-one time with my parents. Not only did I grow up in a big family but we often had extended family staying with us. I think I really would have liked to have that one-on-one time with my parents, less responsibility on my shoulders, and more being able to just be a kid.

Because of my role, my siblings grew up seeing me as a third parent. That warped their relationship with me as a big sister. I never wanted that parent role. It's a weird in-between as a sibling. We might be given the role of a parent, but we don't have the power of a parent. I couldn't discipline or punish them, but they were expected to listen to me. It's a figurehead role that was set up to be unsuccessful. It's also really frustrating because you're still expected to fulfill the duties of a parent with none of the tools. Now that we're older, I play more of a mediator role and less of a parent role to my siblings. I know how to talk to my parents and I also know what my siblings are experiencing and help them see eye to eye on things. I help navigate cultural barriers or typical family conflicts.

Our parents believed strongly in the value of not forgetting who you are and where you come from. Our Islamic studies were very important to them, as well as passing on the culture. We went to dugsi on the weekends and took pride in our faith. We spoke Somali at home, even though my parents could speak English. Even with my own kids, I am intentional about teaching them to be bilingual. My parents will sometimes speak English to my kids, and I have to remind them not to. They complain that my kids won't understand them, but I say they will if they don't have a choice.

My parents showed us love in a physical way through feeding us, clothing us, and putting a roof over our heads. Also by spending time with us. My dad would take us to the toy stores and buy us toys. I loved reading, so he would always take me to the library, no matter how often I wanted to go. And every night that he was home, he would tell us a bedtime story. He created grandiose tales of adventure on the spot, and he would never tell the same story twice.

My mom likewise showed us love by the time that she spent with us. She would take us places and bring us along to visit family. We'd joke around and enjoy each other's laughter. Those are the moments I remember the most. I appreciate that time even more now because I know how much was on their plates. Yet still, they were able to connect with us and spend quality time with us.

My parents did a decent job in treating the girls and boys in our family fairly. Chores were divided pretty equally between us. In terms of expectations for behavior and goals, things weren't that different between us.

There's a pattern I've picked up on in the younger generation like mine. I feel like there's a gap between mother and daughters. Like there's something that's missing. I'm not sure if this is a real phenomenon or something I've perceived. I believe the relationships mothers have with their sons cause that wedge. I haven't been able to fully pinpoint it, but it's something I'm interested in exploring in my research.

My relationship with my mom is ever evolving. We're close, and we talk pretty frequently. She lives in Ohio still. We make it work. We've had bumps along the way. But she's always been someone I can turn to. Now that she's a grandma, it's a whole 'nother ball game. But as a parent, sometimes you just have to put your stuff to the side so that it doesn't impact your kids. This perspective of the gray area has definitely helped. We're all just trying to figure it out, and as we recognize the complexity of our parents and their struggles, let's acknowledge our own and give ourselves credit.

My greatest accomplishments are my kids. I have two daughters and a son, and I put so much intentional work into them. My greatest fear for my children is the world they live in. It's a place that can be very harsh. I can only do so much for so long to protect them from that. And that scares me. And I know it's not healthy to just keep them locked in the house forever. But living in a very terrifying and unsafe world beats you down in a number of different ways. And my fear is, how is that going to impact them? My greatest hope for my kids is that they are content and fulfilled in life. I want them, first and foremost, to please Allah (سبحانه وتعالى). And once they do that, I feel like the other pieces come into play. I pray that they continue to have the traits they have now. I hope that doesn't get diminished in any capacity because these are the really unique things that make them who they are. I love that my older daughter is creative, that my son is inquisitive, and that my youngest daughter has a fire within her. I know as a girl that fire can get dimmed down, but I want her to keep it alive.

～

To Somali people: We are strong people. We need to go back to the traits of our ancestors in their assertiveness and strength. We live in areas that allow us to think we are not capable, but we are very capable.

To Somali women: You are absolutely strong and resilient and you give so much. We give a lot to people. We need to start prioritizing ourselves and empowering ourselves so that we may show up for each other and the people we love.

To Somali men: You are strong and capable. We need more support and action for your sisters. We need to do better by our boys. Raising them and holding space to undo toxic masculinity. Modeling expressing emotions and healthy communication. Instilling a sense of responsibilities. We need you to play an active role in nurturing these traits in our homes.

10

Kaltun Karani, 30s, United Arab Emirates

I was born and raised in the United Arab Emirates, and I am the second-youngest of eight children. Kaltun means either a person with high cheekbones or a garment that people of Jannah wear. My mom named me after the Prophet Muhammad's ﷺ daughter, Umm Kalthoum. In my adolescence, we relocated to Syria. When we moved to Syria, our plan was for our father to eventually join us from Ethiopia. He passed away before he could make it to us, Allahu naxariirsto. We lived in Syria for less than a year because my mother didn't want to start over in a new country without our father. So we went back to Dubai for a few more years before eventually coming to America when I was thirteen years old. I lived in Ohio for many years before making Minnesota home.

~

I loved that during my time in the United Arab Emirates our school system valued Islamic history. It was the foundation for my subsequent career and lifelong appreciation and understanding of Islam. Culturally, I am definitely a Somali Arab. It's in the same way that Somali American kids grew up with American influence or Somali Norwegians grew up with Scandinavian cultural influence.

I identify myself as a Muslim Somali Arab American. I put my faith identity before all my cultural identities. It's in that order because obviously my Islam doesn't change, that's my faith. Somali because that's home, that's who I am. Arab because my first thirteen years of life, that's what I knew. The culture that I grew up in. American because that's the other part of my life. It's the culture I grew up in and that helped form me. I don't usually identify myself as Black. It doesn't come up for me. It's definitely a part of who I am in this culture and society. But it's not automatically the first thing that comes to my mind. We didn't grow up with race the way Americans do. Perhaps I have an issue reconciling between my race and my ethnicity because I see ethnicity as the way I identify myself. Because I grew up in the UAE, where ethnicity is how you identify yourself. You are asked: Are you Arab? Are you Pakistani? Are you Somali? Are you Sudani? Where are you from? It's about the nation you're from. It's jarring because in America the world identifies me as a Black woman.

～

My time in Syria was mixed. I loved the people and the school I went to. During recess, it was normal to see kids fighting, just as it was normal to see kids playing. One day some Syrian kids told me they were gonna beat me up. I told the teacher on them, so they wanted to get back at me. I was scared for my life. I was a chubby kid who didn't know how to fight or run. But the other kids told me, "Don't worry; we have your back." And they really did. Some of them held the kids back. Another one took my backpack. A couple others cheered me on as I ran to my apartment. One kid literally ran ahead and went to the building where we lived just so he could buzz me up and I could run right up the stairs. I got to my apartment without a scratch, all because of those kids. That was a master class in loyalty.

The few months I lived in Syria were emotionally hard. I didn't have my parents or my eldest sister. My dad had passed away, and my mom went back to Dubai to run our family restaurant. I was left in the care of my siblings and my cousins. One of my cousins was very kind, and the other was not. The cruel one was mostly in charge of me. That was my childhood vulnerability.

～

Our parents were not very religious, but they loved the diin. My mom made sure we went to Arabic schools so that we can understand the Qur'an. My dad led by example on prayer and made sure my brothers were always on time to pray. So even though my parents were not particularly religious, my oldest brother had become overzealous. He was young and just getting into the diin. He was trying to find his way but had such harsh interpretations of our faith. I had a best friend in my neighborhood who was Christian, and my brother forbade me to play with her. This was so odd to me. Why would it matter that she's Christian? So I learned to play with my friend when he wasn't around.

Another time, my brother decided that I could wear only black clothes, and they had to be one size bigger for modesty's sake. I was only nine or ten years old. We went to a park, and other children began asking, "Why are you wearing all black?" And one of my loyal Syrian friends defended me by saying, "Be nice to her. Her father just died. That's why she's wearing black." Meanwhile, the other kids were dressed in shorts and colorful clothing. I stuck out like a sore thumb. I was so unhappy and embarrassed. Not only because my clothing looked odd and uncomfortable, but also because it wasn't safe. I nearly died crossing a busy intersection because my skirt was extremely long and I tripped and struggled to get up to save myself. I still remember the fear of cars coming my way as I tried to get unstuck under the long skirt.

On that day, I missed my mom and my sister even more. My sister used to protect me and defend me all the time, especially because she was older than my brother. Whenever my mother would try to dissuade my brother from enforcing his strict rules, he would say, "You let the other sister go without wearing hijab, so I'm not gonna let you do that with Kaltun." It took me a long time to understand why my brother was the way he was with me. Young, impressionable, and passionate about diin, he was trying to make his way through a religion he was just beginning to learn. He had not yet mastered the diin, nor was he mature enough to understand the text and nurture the spiritual development of a child.

〜

Eventually we moved back to Dubai with my mom before immigrating to the United States. We settled in Columbus, Ohio. Before I felt settled, I remember being upset with my mother because every time it felt like we were settling down and I was getting used to a new school and making friends, we would be packing to leave. I felt like my dreams for high school, college, and eventual career kept getting interrupted, and I felt unstable. I graduated from high school and college in Ohio. I ended up making lifelong friends and falling in love with the community there.

I've had the privilege of attending school in different countries. Out of all the places, Dubai was definitely the most comprehensive and rigorous. In the States, I kept thinking, *This can't be learning, it's too easy, where's the catch?* A huge part of that reason is that I was not placed in the right classes in Ohio. One of my biggest issues with the American education system is the belittlement of minority students. Many educators and peers just assume that POC or international students are not as smart. I remember being a senior in high school and being enrolled in ninth-grade math. Nobody assessed my comprehension and skills. They just assumed I was behind. I questioned my mother's thinking behind accepting this and thought, *This is what my mom wants me to get up for every morning? This is what we do in school? Americans are dumb.* Little did I know, they thought I was dumb. My mother didn't know how the system worked, so she couldn't advocate for me.

I did not connect with other students in high school. I remember one kid's remark on the school bus one day. He heard me talking to somebody, and he said, "Oh my God. She speaks English." At my school, I was the only Muslim. I was the only Somali. I was the only one wearing hijab at one point. Another day, I was leaving my government class. I remember talking to my teacher and joking around with him and we were laughing. This girl walked in the classroom. We only saw each other in the hallway. And she looked at me and said, "Oh my God. I didn't know you spoke English." I thought to myself, *why would you assume that?*

The school never took the initiative to bridge the cultural gap between students, so there were a lot of assumptions. I also didn't step out of my comfort zone to make connections. It's a lot to put on a kid, least of all someone new to the country. I was a very social person growing up. In the UAE, in Syria, I had a lot of friends. And then I came to Ohio, and it was like my Mexican friend Erica was the only one I really connected with. She was the only person I became close with. I would say hello to others and have very casual conversations. But to have friends, where we knew each other intimately and we went to one another's homes, I had none besides Erica. That was hard, to not have friends in school. It was not easy for a social person.

~

My peers had a perception of me based on my faith, that maybe I was uber religious, but that wasn't really who I was. I was a Muslim but didn't pray regularly. I went to parties and didn't really wear hijab. I was living day by day; it was all about having fun. Then one day, a few of my friends literally forced me to take an AlMaghrib class. I didn't want to be there, but they paid for it and I had no choice. I couldn't come up with any excuse at that point. I was blown away. I'd never heard Allah (سبحانه وتعالى) being spoken about in that way. I'd never hear Allah (سبحانه وتعالى) being spoken about in terms of mercy, kindness, and compassion. I saw people who were like me but more committed to their diin. And then at the end of the course, the instructor told us to prepare for the course test, because the exam is compulsory. The teacher was so cool, and he offered to be a mentor to those who did well in the exam, so I committed in my mind to take the exam. He also reminded us that the real test was on the day we would stand in front of Allah (سبحانه وتعالى). This second part completely changed the way I lived my life. That's when my relationship with my faith began. I continued taking courses, and in the next ten years I earned a degree in Islamic studies.

In high school, I was unhappy and completely disengaged. I did the bare minimum. I really think that for students to succeed in high school, positive relationships are important. And the relationships with peers are really important to young people. So how do we make sure that our youth have positive relationships at school and in life?

For one thing, we need more teachers of color. I have fond memories of them. One stood out in particular: an African American teacher, Mr. Wagstaff. He took it upon himself to stand by my locker with me and explain African American history to me. I knew very little about African American history, and I hadn't learned much of it in a classroom. But this teacher would tell me things about segregation, about what it was like to be an African American fifty or a hundred years before. I really appreciated him. I had another teacher in an information technology vocational program in high school. He could tell I was a demotivated type of student. I would routinely cut class. I had no motivation to just get up and go to school because I wasn't challenged or engaged. This teacher sat down with me one day and said, "Kaltun, what's really going on with you? You're missing a lot of school. Is everything okay?" I was touched that he approached me with good intentions to check in on me and sincerely wanted to help.

I skipped high school graduation because I was so ready to be done with it all. I never wanted to set foot in that school again if I didn't have to. One of my friends said to me, "Kaltun, they called your name three times at the graduation ceremony." And I was like, I'm so glad they did that, so that everybody knows I graduated.

∽

My journey to college had a lot of obstacles. I went to my high school counselor one day and said to him, "Everyone I'm around is talking about taking the SAT test. What is it, and do I need to be preparing?" He told me, "You don't need to take that. You are going to community college." I heard "college" and said yes, I need to go to college. But I didn't understand this. In hindsight, he was giving me a ceiling. Another time I went to him and said, "I'm supposed to be graduating. I'm not supposed to be in tenth grade. What do I need to do to get out of here?" And he said, "You can go to the tech school." And the tech school was basically where you send students who are interested in vocational training and getting a job after high school, not necessarily going to college.

I ended up enrolling in this technical vocational program, and it really became the best part of my school experience. I felt like I was finally learning, being challenged, and I enjoyed it more than the remedial classes the school staff had presumptuously placed me in. But at the same time, I didn't realize until years later that my counselor thought I didn't have the ability for a rigorous, academic career. I graduated from high school; I went to Columbus State Community College. And then I transferred to The Ohio State University and was in business school.

I went back to visit my counselor because I was in the Somali student association. At this time, I was an accounting major. When I went to see him, he called everyone in the office and said, "Can you believe she went to the tech school?" He was just so incredulous about my academic advancement that it finally dawned on me that he didn't think I could do it. He made a lot of assumptions about my ability. And he was a nice guy! He was very friendly and well meaning, but he really never checked how his assumptions and bias were limiting his students. I am glad I was a naive student, because had I understood and internalized his limitations for me, I would have limited my academic and career ambition and success. It is so crucial for educators to question their judgment of student ability, because whether they realize it or not, their judgment limits their students' performance. They end up not challenging the students enough so they can academically succeed.

It's hard for our folks to challenge adults like these counselors or teachers because we come from a culture where the adults are always right and not meant to be questioned. The counselors won't straight-up call a student stupid; they just heavily imply it in different ways. My friend Erica also went to the community college. She transferred to a four-year university. She always had a job and took care of her family. And when she graduated from the four-year university, she said to me, "Can you believe I did it?" And I was like, "Of course! Why would I not believe that?" And then I realized that both she and I were in the vocational training program. That she assumed we were not college material. We were not supposed to do higher education. But here we are: I graduated from the university, and so did she. If you're young and you grew up in this American educational system, you internalize all the things the teachers and counselors and administrators think about you. It took a lot for me to get in touch with my inner truth and wisdom.

～

The pressure to have it figured out at age eighteen in order to choose a career is unrealistic. Especially when you have not been given the tools of self-knowledge and career knowledge. This is why I had multiple changes in my undergraduate program. I first thought I was going to go into computer science because I loved my high school IT program. Then I applied to business school and had a major in finance. Then I decided to do accounting. Halfway through accounting, I realized I really didn't like it, so I switched to marketing. I was three semesters away from graduating and didn't want to waste my credits, but I also realized at that point that had I known myself better, I would have majored in social work. My entire undergrad experience was just going with the flow, going off of other people's advice and with the pressure to just finish because that's how it's "supposed" to be.

After I graduated, I started a journey of self- and career discovery. I was working at Verizon Wireless and had already done an internship in the marketing department. Since I had a marketing degree, this of course made logical sense. I was good at sales too, but I knew it wasn't for me. I didn't feel fulfilled in my work. I left Verizon and got a job as a parent liaison and teacher assistant. I've worked all sorts of jobs in education. I was a substitute teacher, a preschool teacher, and an informal counselor to students and parents. I learned a lot and connected well with the kids. I also saw educational disparities in the Somali community. I worked in a mental health organization doing psychiatric community support, and here I saw the mental health needs of the Somali community.

When I moved to Minnesota, I worked as an early childhood coach, and I learned a lot about what it looks like to have quality interactions with children so they can succeed in school and life. That's why I am in school for my master's in school counseling. I'm really passionate about giving kids all the tools they need to succeed and live happy, healthy lives. I knew I was in the right field because I combined what I liked over the years and found my place. It brought together the educational setting, the collaborating with parents and staff, and counseling students on their well-being and success. I didn't wake up one day and say, "This is what I'll be." It took a lot of trial and error.

Kids at the school where I'm doing my internship asked me, "Did you imagine yourself doing this?" That's a good question. We don't come from a culture where we ask, "what do you want to be when you grow up?" I think in the culture I grew up in, the Arab culture, women were prepared for marriage and parenting more than for a career. I remember my friends were surprised when they saw my mom driving or my mom working. They were like, "Your mom does this? Our mom doesn't do that." There were already expectations in place. I grew up in that particular culture. I also grew up with the influence of a Somali mom who worked hard to take care of her children as a single parent. She valued education and independence for me more than anything. I still remember her panic when she realized I was talking to a guy when I was eighteen. She sat me at the dinner table and asked me if I wanted marriage or education. She wanted me to prioritize education, and I did that. I didn't want to disappoint my mom at all.

∾

I'm really grateful that a lifetime of experience helped build my appreciation and understanding of the diin. I don't think as a community we nurture that in women. I remember my dad would make sure my brothers went to the masjid, but I wasn't included. I don't think anybody said, "Is Kaltun praying?" I don't think we as a community see women's religious scholarship as something significant or important or something worth developing. We don't. We see women going into education, secular education, becoming professionals, but not teachers of Islam.

The first time I was asked to speak in a conference, a Somali woman told me it was unacceptable for me to speak publicly. She asked, "Why do you have to speak? Why can't the men speak? There are a lot of men who can do this. Why do you have to do it?" That's coming from a seventy-plus-year-old person, an elder. There's the cultural notion that this work is for men. I think unfortunately we do come from a very misogynistic culture. But unless we disrupt that or we create the avenue, we risk raising another generation of girls who feel left out of their faith tradition.

∼

I started Hikma Academy in 2014. Since I had my son, I didn't want to work full-time anymore. I also wanted a way to study the Qur'an more in depth and teach it more than is possible at a halaqa. A halaqa is more of a general, public, and casual reminder. Instead, I wanted a community of students who had the same goals. I launched Hikma Academy with the idea of creating a spiritual home for girls and women. One of my friends asked if I could start a group for her and a small group of adult women. I didn't have the confidence to teach adults at the time—it was intimidating. But I took a leap of faith and put my best foot forward. Hikma Academy students became my extended family. My teenage students became my daughters, and my adult students became my soul sisters. I developed deep friendships and had the privilege of mentoring young girls. It changed my life.

We've been able to hold classes, retreats, and events for women and girls. During our retreats we play all types of games and activities, and the girls get to share their feelings, thoughts, and questions in a safe space. I would give them the opportunity to do presentations on topics important to them, and we would explore it together and embed Islam into it. They would discuss mental health issues, marriage, gender, issues affecting boys, issues affecting girls, race, culture, and just about everything under the sun. The conversations weren't censored or contrived; it was very organic and raw. We're building confidence and trust in these girls through sisterhood and showing them that people care about them. It's such an important space to create, because I know I didn't have that space growing up, and a lot of women and girls can relate. I was so touched when one of my students called me her third mom.

For some of them, these classes are the first positive experience of Islamic education. They were learning the meaning of what they had memorized at a young age and seeing what it meant to live the wisdom found in the Qur'an and Sunnah. Those relationships are lifelong, even though the classes are not. But when the course ends, these girls have built such a bond that they continue to meet with one another. We get together every once in a while, and it makes my heart glow to see them grow up in front of my eyes. Now they're going into college and they're facing a whole new world with new challenges: mental health, loneliness, identity issues, social issues, and so on and so forth. The value of having these programs for girls is that they aren't going through these issues alone. During these hyper-isolated times, a community of girls and trusted mentors can make a world of difference. My dream is to build up the resources to be able to provide that.

I'm glad I found the courage to follow that dream and found Hikma Academy. It reminds me of Hodan Nalayeh, Allahu naxariisto. She created a platform for Somalis all over the diaspora and made content that challenged the perception of Somalia. She did that by storytelling. I'm very proud of the legacy she left behind and hope she inspires the next generation of Somali youth.

～

I had a friend who was always telling me to "move to Minnesota. It's got better opportunities. It's got better jobs." He really believed in my potential and career. I appreciated it, but I knew I wasn't going to leave my mom's place without being married. He later introduced me to the man I would eventually marry. In our culture, we're accustomed to move where your husband lives. Now I had my reason. My husband had an established career in Minnesota, so I made the move.

Marriage is beautiful, and it is also a test. It provides you the opportunity for major inner growth. We don't talk about how to be a wife. We don't talk about how to be a husband. And then, here you are. You're expected to mesh together. Alhamdulilah, if there is love and kindness and respect for one another, you'll make it through. But there are so many challenges. How do you simply communicate? How do you tell this person, "this is how I'm feeling"? How do you define boundaries? There's a learning curve that no one prepares you for. One thing I didn't expect were the cuddles. They were the sweetness of marriage. It's so beautiful to share this connection and to build intimacy. After I had given birth, my husband helped me shower and dress and took care of me in my most vulnerable state. Being married takes mercy, a lot of kindness and respect, intimacy, and a bond. It's something you spend a lifetime building.

My husband is an amazing father. He's very disciplined and organized, unlike myself. He carries that personality into his fathering style. Whenever he mows the lawn or takes out the trash, he tells our son Imran to complete a task. We're pretty divided in terms of chores. But when I tell Imran to put shoes away or something, I have to use a lot of motivational tactics. When his father tells him, he just does it. Sometimes I look from the window and see Imran and his dad raking leaves together and it puts a smile on my face. I'm insanely grateful. I love that they get to do things together, even if it's just chores. In our community, we often notice boys when they act out as teenagers or later in life. We need quality parenting before it even gets to that level. As first-generation immigrants, we're in survival mode so much that it's hard to find time to be intentional. But it's really important for fathers to spend that quality time with their children, especially with their sons. Play together, go to the beach, just go and hang out. Build trust and friendship and show your kids you care by making time for them. We have to show love and support to have a positive influence and before problems arise.

Marriage is also about finding and appreciating the ways your partner communicates love. I had a moment when I was hung up on conversations because my expectations were not working out. I crave emotional intimacy, and speech is one of my love languages. My husband shows love through service. He's so considerate and caring. And I eventually saw those things and felt the blessing. Don't get hung up about what it ought to be or what you expected. Take that time to get to know each other and step outside of yourself. And pray for a man with good character and good diin. Yes, we have our share of challenges; every marriage does. This is why I am always making dua for my marriage and the quality of my marriage.

～

Kids are a tremendous source of joy. It also takes a lot of responsibility to be an effective parent and caretaker. Quality of education is a serious predictor of quality of life. One of the best lessons I learned in school was about finding balance with education. I had a teacher tell me to balance fun with seriousness. I think she really figured me out and was then able to give me sincere advice. I tend to not apply myself as much as I could. I tend to enjoy life and, you know, chill. If I took myself more seriously, I would have been where I wanted to be sooner. So have fun and take your education seriously. Take your learning seriously. Take your commitments seriously.

My aunt, who is over eighty, tells me, "God has given you your children, but they don't belong to you." This is Somali wisdom. My aunt said this to me because she saw me hugging and kissing my son and being affectionate with him. She thought it was too much, because where she came from, she needed to not be so attached because many babies and children often died. Her generation experienced a lot of loss, so they put up a wall to protect themselves. I took her wisdom with my own twist. Your job is to take care of your children and prepare them for life, not to be emotionally attached to their existence or success. Give your kids love and know that you're doing the best to take care of them, but also be aware that you're not in control. And if you're tested through your kids, don't internalize it as your failure as a person. Our job is to train our children to make the best choices. We cannot force them to make the choices we want. We have to give them the tools to think, to know how to fix mistakes and to feel empowered.

The beauty of parenting is that it is what you make it. Parenting is not something you can outsource. You can't hold other people accountable for your kids, because they are your greatest responsibility and blessing. The harshness that we see in our culture of parenting is not in the favor of our kids. Bullying a kid to know their culture will not get the results you're expecting. You don't send your child to preschool and expect the teacher to beat him into discipline. Effective teachers are assertive and kind. They praise and celebrate the children. How, then, do we expect that putting children down will strengthen them? How do we also expect them to love Qur'an and diin and send them to a teacher who is holding the punishment stick? Of course they would develop an unhealthy relationship with the Qur'an and faith, unless Allah (سبحانه وتعالى) saves them from that. We must be patient and kind if we want to see them patient and kind. We must heal the parts of ourselves that carry wounds we may pass to our children. It's our responsibility to pass on to our children the best way of being. We have the best intention as parents. Do we have access to the best methods?

I have a friend who packed up her life in the States and moved to an African country. She's a mother, and she thought the best thing for her to do was to take her kids out of the country and raise them in a place where they see themselves, where they see Black everywhere. She wants to prevent them from developing Black inferiority from isolation. That was her solution. Another person's solution might be immersing their kids in a Black environment stateside. I'm gonna send my kids to urban schools. I want them to be around people who are like them. Another person might use books as a tool. They will teach their kids Black history that will help build their character and strengthen them. There's no shortage of ways that Black parents are trying to prepare their kids for the world.

～

I was highly emotional during Brett Kavanaugh's controversial confirmation hearing for his seat on the Supreme Court. Dr. Christine Blasey Ford not being believed stood out to me. This was around the time my daughter was born. I started reflecting on what fears and hopes I had when my son was born. For my son, I feared a world that would kill him or kill his spirit. I prayed for him to have joy in this life and in the next life. For my daughter, I prayed she would become a strong woman. I was afraid of a world that abuses women sexually, mentally, emotionally, or physically. This is something I continue to think and reflect upon.

I gave birth to my daughter, and everything was okay for a while. After four months, strange things started happening. I started hallucinating. I was telling my friends I couldn't sleep. I remember thinking that I was evil and I needed to remove myself from all the circles where I had positive influence.

I wrote a message in a group chat that alarmed my friend who is a therapist. She called me and said, "Kaltun, this is not typical for you; you sound flat and different; you don't sound like yourself." I had told her how I was having a hard time sleeping and couldn't go to the doctor because I didn't have health insurance. She convinced me to call a postnatal hotline and use the screening metric to assess what was going on. I called my clinic and spoke to a nurse who said, "You sound like you need to come into the hospital." They thought I was experiencing postpartum depression. However, I was so confused and delirious that I couldn't communicate with my mother or husband that I needed to go to the hospital. I then lost consciousness and could no longer advocate for myself. Over the next two or three days, my mother and husband tried their best to keep me rested and sleeping. I wasn't sleeping. They tried to use sleeping pills and herbal and spiritual methods to get me to sleep. Because I have a sibling with a mental illness, my mother was terrified of the idea of going to a hospital. I became more and more delusional.

My best friend had just returned from a trip, and when she saw me in that state, she made plans with my husband to take me to the hospital. I remember glimpses of that experience. Some of those moments make me laugh because it was just hilarious what I was thinking, saying, and doing. Some are terrifying and extremely traumatizing. I was diagnosed with the severe and rare condition of postpartum psychosis. I was in the hospital for two weeks. I don't remember much of it, but I remember feeling confused, not knowing who I was or where I was, forgetting my children, and even forgetting my date of birth. My husband and my best friend visited me every day. Toward the end of my stay, my husband brought me printed pictures of my kids. I put them on the windows in my hospital room. I feel like those pictures pulled me out of whatever darkness my mind went to.

I had the full support of my husband and my best friend, who became my sister. My mom, who uses a walker, was caring for my four-month-old baby. I was blessed with friends who showed up to help my mom, to care for my son, and to support me once I came back home. The depression after the psychosis was deep and long. This illness was the biggest test I've ever experienced. I pray I never experience it again.

As I was healing, I started talking to my friends about what I had experienced. And so many women told me about their postpartum depression or anxiety. Many women experience these illnesses, but seeking help in the form of therapy, group support, or medication is not common, given mental health stigma and mistrust of the mental health profession. Can you imagine how many women are isolated in their struggle as a result? There is also a stigma about even talking about it. So you might question yourself: "Is this a thing that happens to women or is something wrong with me?" And it's also about new motherhood and being good enough.

There's so much pressure on a new mom. About being able to handle everything and not ask for help. It's unfair and unrealistic. I remember two weeks after I had given birth to my daughter, I was sitting in grad school finishing up my last semester of classes. I had speaking engagements that I was excited about. I published my first book and was having a launch party. Two months after my baby was born, my husband also traveled for two weeks, and I was taking care of everything. My therapist, my family, and my friends all said that I was doing too much for a new mom. But I wasn't buying it. I learned a lot from this experience, and one thing that I will forever prioritize is my own sleep and self-care.

~

I learned something about my community in high school. During my senior year, there was a huge influx of Somali kids. Some of them were from Egypt. We formed a group and hung out, ate lunch together, and had each other's backs. We made the mistake one day of standing in the White area. We were having a blast, cracking jokes, and doing teenage things. Then one White kid came over and picked a fight with us. One of the Somali kids absolutely refused to stand for it. He was like, "You can't belittle me like that." The interesting thing for me is that you're supposed to keep your head down. That was the unspoken rule in this country. But my friends and I came to this country already grown. I was in high school when I arrived. We weren't conditioned to back down and not talk back, to keep our heads down and stay out of trouble. We weren't taught to hide and shrink ourselves, to hide our personalities. We are people who have pride. Cultural pride can be a shield, but it can also be an Achilles' heel.

I think this is a part of why our country is at war too. Because pride is a double-edged sword. It's good to be prideful, to be proud of yourself and your heritage and your culture. To value yourself, see yourself, and have a positive self-image. That's the way we should be as human beings. God created us like that. But at the same time, humble yourself. And have some humility in some areas. I think that, as a people, we have pride without humility sometimes. And this is why there's constant fighting. "My tribe is better than yours. My family's better than yours. I am better than you. I will lead you; I will not follow you." That's a disease of the heart.

~

My mom eventually made the big move to Minnesota years after me. She was shortly followed by one of my brothers and his family. I'm so grateful to have them here; now I'm not as lonely. I have a super strong attachment to Mom since my father's passing. That was the hardest part of moving to Minnesota. I didn't know what life would be like here. I didn't have my friends and my family. It was even harder when I had my children and my mother wasn't around. Or she would visit intermittently. When my mother lived in Ohio, I went back four or five times every year. When she moved here, I went back only a couple times for weddings. Now my friends visit me here, and I've slowly planted seeds in their minds to move here. Minnesota is a great state. There are more opportunities here. The community is thriving.

When my mom moved to Minnesota, she settled in Cedar-Riverside. I've tried for years to convince my mother to move in with me. She insists on living there. The most important thing that I worry about is her living on her own. She's gotten older. She had to stop driving a few years ago because it became unsafe. She totaled her car in Ohio and fought me on giving up driving, but it had to stop. But now that she can't drive, it's hard for me to drive her places because I've got two little kids. And I worry about her. But she doesn't want to give up that independent life. I remember I sat my mom down one day and told her that I think it's time that she moves in with me, and she actually cried. It was so painful. It was a really hard conversation because, in her mind, she thought I was complaining and that she was a burden. I did not want her to be alone and unsafe. Back home you had generations of families living together and looking after each other. Here in America, you've only got yourself. The American family structure is so isolated and lonely. If my mom lived with me or any of my siblings, the kids would have their grandma and we could properly look after her instead of juggling two households.

But she has valid reasons as well. I live in the suburbs. The Cedar neighborhood is in the city, and she has lots of other Somali elders and companions, as opposed to the isolation of a suburb. She also doesn't want to lose the comfort of her own space. Many of our elders don't want to live with the son-in-law. I have another brother who lives here, but he has a lot of kids. And his plate is extremely full. So it really means that I'm the one; I'm the primary caretaker of my mom. And that is both a blessing and a responsibility, and I'm trying to make it work.

There's a generation of us experiencing our parents aging and what that care entails. Our parents don't have savings or retirement income. Their children are their retirement plan. In a perfect world, this would be a sure thing, but we're by no means wealthy. Some of us are trying to make ends meet, pay off student loans, juggle kids, or meaningfully advance. We're not living the American dream of gold-paved roads. This is the reality. For me personally, it's hard to navigate these responsibilities. I'm a mother, wife, caretaker, and student, with a career. What am I sacrificing or renegotiating so that I can meet my priorities? It's a constant tug and pull.

I want Somali girls to learn their faith. I think there is a whole lot of injustice happening in the world toward women. If you really study Islam, you're going to see the wisdom of Allah (سبحانه وتعالى). The Prophet ﷺ has empowered us. But when we're ignorant about our faith, we're going to live in that injustice if we don't empower ourselves and study. There are even Muslim scholars who said things about women that are unjust. How can we discern that if we don't know the religion? Nobody's going to do it for you. You can't outsource your faith. And if you study it, you will become a more confident Muslim. You'll raise more confident children, Muslim children. I offer the same to our Somali men. Study your diin and be kind.

11

Shamis Ibrahim, 40s, Mogadishu, Somalia

pseudonym

I was born in Mogadishu during arguably one of Somalia's best times. We gained our independence from colonialists and our nation began to define who we would be. I attended school in Mogadishu until I finished middle school. After that, our family moved. I lived in Kenya and France before immigrating to the United States as a young woman.

I am the youngest of seven. I have four brothers and two sisters; one brother has passed away. Before Somalia developed an official language, we had multiple schools with different language focus for students. You could study Arabic or Italian, among other languages. My older brother took Italian, my sister took English, and the rest of my siblings took Arabic. In 1973, Somali became the official language, and we began to learn how to write in Somali. I was in kindergarten when select schools started teaching Somali language and script, and I was among the first to start studying it. For my siblings it was too late; they had to finish school in the language studies they already started. I'm grateful to have been at the right place and right time for that educational and historic opportunity.

My parents were very intentional about their roles and our upbringing. My mom was a stay-at-home mom. She didn't have the hectic and fatiguing lifestyle of running from place to place, being everything all at once. We never had a babysitter. She was very proud about being fully present for her children. The best thing she ever did for me was to not allow anyone else to raise me. My older sister was my mom's caretaker before she passed. My sister told me my mom used to say, "I have never left my children for someone else to babysit; I never let my children be taken care of by other people. If I go to the store, I take them. If I go anywhere, I take them. Whatever I was doing, my children would come with me." And I think that's the most beautiful thing. I wish I had known that. Whenever we came home from school, our mom was there to greet us. If we didn't see our mom, the house felt empty. Every aunt, cousin, and kid could be at my house, but if Mom wasn't there, it didn't feel like home. My mom did everything for us. She looked after us, cooked, and cleaned. Moms are the cherishers, sustainers, and nurturers. My mom was a superhero.

Dad was the provider, protector, discipliner, and healer. If I needed anything, I would go to my dad. If I needed a doctor, clothes, or something for school, I went straight to him because I knew he was the provider. My dad had a prestigious job. He used to travel a lot. He would bring us gifts and souvenirs from overseas. We would brag to our friends, "My jeans are from Italy."

When the news first broke out about trouble with the government, our family was told to move from our house. Dad was arrested and jailed by the new Siad Barre regime but luckily was released. Anyone associated with the old administration was viewed with suspicion. Not everyone who was detained got out alive. My sister broke down crying. This great big house was our childhood home and a special place. Our dad's career afforded us a comfortable lifestyle; we had a driver who would take us to school. It was a big home and a big life. My sister asked him, "Where are we gonna go? Where are we gonna live?" My dad looked at her and said, "Look, as long as I breathe and I live, I'm gonna build you a bigger home and better place." And he kept his promise. We ultimately were able to return to the same neighborhood. The new president eventually called my dad, and he was given a new job and a diplomatic passport.

Somali parents are very, very caring. I have a great deal of sympathy for them and give them extra credit. That generation left the war, left behind their homes, didn't know what life would be, got educated, worked hard, and raised families in a new country. And then their children believe that their parents know nothing. "You don't understand." But they understand more than you think. Because if the situation was reversed, could the children do what their parents did?

～

Dugsi was a huge part of my childhood. That's Somali DNA. If a child doesn't go to dugsi, something's wrong. We went every morning. My mom would take us early most days. She would open all the windows in the home and badger us to get out of bed. She didn't like us sleeping in late. After dugsi in the morning, we attended school in the afternoon. The school used to be in two groups. Morning group would go at 7:00, and they left at lunch. And then lunch and the second group, and they would leave at 6:00. We were taught by two brothers. We liked the younger one better because he would let us play between ashar. Dugsi teachers were like second parents. It's very loving. They weren't excessive, and they didn't give parents something to worry about. They had the best interests of their students in mind, like parents have for their kids. You would fear your macalin like your own parents.

Diin is very important to our culture. The beauty of faith is that it is a matter of the heart; you don't need to be an intellectual to be moved by it. And you don't have to burden yourself by pretending to know everything. We can stay in our lanes. Doubts are a powerful thing. If you open that door, you will overanalyze because you're not equipped. That's a difficult place to be. Faith isn't physical; you can't see it, touch it, or smell it. You feel it with your heart.

I've been in the United States for many years. I don't plan on going back to Somalia. I'm not sure if I will. I hear people say, "I want to go back to Mogadishu. I want to go home." I never truly said that from my heart. I don't believe in giving my heart to any place. A home for me is the home that I grew up in and came from. The moment I left Mogadishu and started traveling, I never had a home. That's not a sad thing to me, because I never had an attachment to one place. I'm in America now because I like to be here; it's my home now. It's where I live, work, and exist. But other than that, it's not my true home. I never think dunya is my home. Wherever I go, I make myself a home. If I had to pick up and leave today, it would require work in a physical sense, but I'm prepared to do it. If I didn't have this perception, it might've been harder for me to come here in the first place.

President Trump has uncovered the hidden beliefs of many people. Before him, you might ask someone, "What do you think about these immigrants coming to America?" and they might say, "Oh, no problem. I like them. They're my neighbors." They've buried or hidden their true feelings, but deep down, it's been boiling for a long time. And then, eventually, someone came into power and said, "Ah, don't be afraid. Let me lift that. Let it boil free." That's all he did. He just took the cover off. And now it's just like a volcano, because people can come out and say how they really feel without having to sugarcoat or excuse it. Now they can say what they want without fear, because they see so many people around them supporting it. They know they're not alone.

I'm not surprised. Those beliefs are ingrained at an early age. We have a similar tribalism in our culture. Everyone has a right to their opinion, but they can't force others to it. Why are you afraid of someone taking your country? If I know I've gotten where I am by taking somebody else's home, then I will always be afraid. Somebody else will come to take my home, right? The fear is in control. It's a fear of the future, because what comes next is unpredictable. For example, if I wronged you, every time I look at you, I think you're gonna do something to me. And you may not do anything to me; you might not even think that I've wronged you. But I will always have that fear. So I always have to tell other people, "Watch her. I don't like her." That's the power of fear.

Fear is a good way to control others. It's an old tactic used to keep people in line. Each side knows what they're capable of, and they project that on to others. They want you to live in fear like they do. But that's no way to live. We can't let fear make our decisions for us. I'm not going to stop wearing hijab because someone might be violent toward me. What's worse is when you begin doubting your diin because of that fear. It's allowing other people's fear and beliefs to determine your own. When you stop wearing hijab or praying your salat because it's dangerous to practice your religion, that's when you open yourself up to something more dangerous. Just say Alhamdulilah, I woke up today. Focus on what you can do, not what you can't. What you can do is what builds you. What you can't is what takes you down. So, focus on what you can.

~

I was married once before, but we went our separate ways. I would love to answer why it didn't work out because there's nothing hidden. It was not my fault, nor his. It's just a relationship where you go and then you grow separate, and then nobody is at fault. Or put differently, everyone carries a bit of the responsibility. But you don't dwell on it. You don't make it the center of your life or victimize yourself. It's just a part of life. Just like how you can grow together, you can also grow apart. No one's the villain, and everyone is the villain. Everybody has their own bad habit. But either you learn from it or you stick with your mistakes. And say, "Oh, no, no, no. It's the other person." No, nothing is wrong with the other person. But there is something wrong with an inability to be accountable.

Here's a surprising thing for those just starting their relationships. Early on, you might be in love, but it could also just be fascination. It's an infatuation. You can overlook signs you are not compatible, or you might convince yourself that he is not as he appears. Then you get married, and the fantasy you created meets reality. That's not the other person's mistake. That's my mistake. All along, that person was exactly the same. But I refused to look at it.

For anyone who wants to get married, take your time. I don't mean delaying marriage; I mean to allow other people to have their opinion. Allow your partner to express and say how they feel. Don't go into marriage by touting independence. A man must have his space. You should allow a man to be a man. But when you are the breadwinner and pay all the bills, how can he be the provider? How can he fulfill his role when he is emasculated? It's how some of us are raised; it's from a place of survival. You know how to take care of yourself, you're proud that you pay the bills and don't need a man, you can't compromise or hear a different opinion; you're married, but you live like you're still single. It's not about finances; it's about two people coming together. If a man is taken from his manhood, there is no relationship. This is a marriage; you need each other. You need to learn how to rely on and trust one another.

The hardest part about marriage is unity. That means, when you're married, it's not just about what you bring to the table. It's what *we* bring to the table. You must let go of egos and allow the other person to come in. "This is how I used to do things; this is how we will do things." It's a joint decision, a partnership. Everyone has flaws, but people are 80 percent or 90 percent good on other things. Don't get caught up in the bad parts. Because the moment you focus on that part, your home is gonna be gone. No one can ever convince you the other 90 percent is good. Because that is the lens you see your spouse through.

My parents taught me a lot about marriage and family through example. They balanced each other out. Whenever my dad would go up a notch, Mom would go down a notch. When he was unhappy or angry about something, she would calm him down. She didn't further inflame the situation. My dad would do the same for my mom when she was angry. They never fought in front of us. They hashed things out in private. They never even had an argument in front of the kids. My parents were like anyone else; they had their good days and bad days. But they were very intentional about protecting us from matters that did not concern us. They let each other have their days. My mom would say, "Okay, today is your day, but tomorrow is mine." They didn't rile each other up, magnify each other's shortcomings, or use it against each other. They didn't allow the little things to stress them out and take away from the bigger picture. My parents had patience for one another. My mom let my dad be the head of the household. She listened to my dad to understand where he was coming from, from the perspective of a man. When they talked, he might say, "Okay, okay, okay." And she could see that as, "What do you mean, 'okay, okay, okay'? Do you hear me?" But "okay" was just his way of showing he was listening. Just because someone is do-

ing something differently, it doesn't mean they're wrong or don't
care. Learn to give the benefit of the doubt.

~

I came to America as a young woman. I moved to Virginia and
lived with my brother. In Kenya, we were taught English, so I
knew the language well before I came to America. I was young
and looking for work before I enrolled in college. I heard from
people that there was work from the US government. In Virginia, the military was recruiting Somali interpreters for a program to help Somalis back home. They said it was for famine
relief, and we were going to help. It was called Operation Re-
store Hope. Of course, the first thing I thought was, "Yes, I want
to go back and help." This was when the war was breaking out,
and we were hearing about the struggle and the chaos people
were seeing back home.

I was on a team of Somali men and women interpreters who
went on the mission. Some of us were assigned to the army;
others air force or marines. And at that time, I was assigned to a
group called CID, the Criminal Investigative Division. I was assigned to the army. There were four of us, and our job was to
investigate.

I'll never forget the day we landed. I was excited to be back
home. I grew up in Mogadishu; I knew every corner of the city. I
made memories on those streets; it's where I was raised. But when
we landed, my stomach was in knots. I sensed that something
was not quite right. I felt this fear of the unknown. I couldn't
recognize my city. It was destroyed. Mogadishu, our nation's legacy, stood in rubble.

We were issued supplies. We had our blankets for sleeping,
our uniforms, MREs, and a backpack. And of course, a bullet-
proof vest. That reminded us we were in a war. The uniform was
a Desert Storm uniform. We had gray or tan khakis, military
boots, and a helmet. At that time, I didn't wear hijab. We looked
exactly like the American soldiers. The only thing I didn't have
was a gun.

We were near the airport, which was connected to the US
embassy in Somalia and a university. We had tents and slept on

cots. The men had their own tents, and we had ours. Some tents had both men and women, but ours was all female. The building was secure from the outside, but once inside, you could move freely. At the beginning of the operation, the marines were in charge, but eventually the army took over.

Even though we worked for the Department of Defense, we were civilians and therefore had civilian rank, which is different from military rank. We were not under the same command and did not have to obey their rank. Regardless, we followed their call, but we were not held to the same very strict military code. For example, as a civilian, I could do mostly whatever I wanted. I could wear my hat whichever way or change my uniform. But a military-rank person could not. So we interpreters got away with a lot of stuff they could not. If the soldiers saw us wearing something differently, they immediately knew we were interpreters.

Our itinerary changed from day to day, so we went where we were needed. We were up by sunrise, and breakfast was at 6:30. I would head to the CID office. That's where we would get our agenda for the day. Mainly, CID would monitor its own soldiers to make sure they were not breaking any codes of conduct or doing something wrong. The CID is supposed to make sure that rules are being met and the community we're serving is not being harmed. That's where the interpreters come in. If a soldier mistreats a Somali civilian, it was our office's job to investigate and monitor conduct. Obviously, they can't speak directly with the community, so that was our job. For example, someone might say a soldier broke into my home and destroyed my property; this is a complaint handled by the CID. We handled many cases that I remember vividly, but because of my security clearance and nondisclosure agreement, I can't speak about them.

The army had a mixed racial makeup. While most soldiers were White, we also saw Black and Hispanic soldiers too. If any Americans looked down on us or treated us with prejudice, it wasn't something I would accept. I was raised to have confidence and to not allow anyone to wrong me, so I knew how to respond with a moment's notice. I grew up with the greatness of Mogadishu, had seen the world, and was not raised to be afraid of or defer to anyone. This is a foreign concept to me.

I came into my own there as a fully formed individual. No one can tell me who I am or what I can or can't do. I knew there was no limit to what I could accomplish. And I would never let anyone victimize me or allow them to make me think anything about myself. You can be shaped by others in that way only if you don't already know yourself. I don't find this attitude unique to just myself. Somali people also share this confidence and sureness about themselves. I think it's a blessing from God and a quality I love about Somalis. I cherish my culture and people, and I know confidently that I don't want to come from anyone but Somalis.

Allah (سبحانه وتعالى) has blessed me to be a Somali. Perhaps I didn't know that when I was younger, but I'm sure of it now. My strength is a gift given to me by God. When I look at our community, I know what I admire is not an arrogance or to say that Somalis are better than other people—never that. I admire the spirit of Somalis that says, "I will not allow you to use or do me any kind of way."

In many ways, we are proud of our culture and who we are. We've had a lot of time in the diaspora to change our names to assimilate or water down our culture to be accepted, but we haven't done that. Somalis have always been a nomadic people who have moved from place to place. We are a people who will find a way and adapt to any circumstance. We can go anywhere, and we will bring our full selves along.

I have to acknowledge how unattached we are as well. If you take me to a random place and say, "You're spending the night here," the first thing I'll say is, "Okay. Where is the bed? Where is the towel? What's for dinner?" I'm okay. I'm not worried about how I will get by or what will happen tomorrow when I wake up. I'm not gonna concern myself about it, because that's how we are; it's in our DNA. We are nomads; we travel. Every home is a temporary home until our next destination. It's the origin of our people. We're like camels. Camels travel for miles and miles with nothing except the humps on their backs. When they have food, they eat. When they have water, they drink. But in the meantime, they carry on. I think of the places I have traveled to and never once thought, *What if?* My American friends and colleagues would ask in shock, "You came to the States by yourself? With no parents or financial security?" And it's not something that even came to mind for me. Instead, I would say, "Why not?" The moment I was a certain age, I was given that permission. There was an understanding that it's my life. It was expected that I find my way. It's not something that has to be said; it's intrinsic. Generation after generation, we moved when it was time to go. I'm still carrying that in me. The ability to survive. And that survival technique is the essence of a Somali.

I remember the day Black Hawk Down happened. We were all sitting outside. The incident happened under Operation Gothic Serpent. It was during a weekday, but the mission, like most missions, happened at night. We were woken up in the middle of the night. There was chaos and panic; it felt like the whole city was awake. Soon after, we were evacuated. The mission was over.

∾

When I came back to America, I enrolled in university. Back then, tuition was very expensive. I didn't get financial aid, and I didn't get help from family. I worked full-time and paid for tuition by myself. I worked for a large company in their manufacturing site. I would go to work at 4:00 PM and work until 1:00 AM. I would run home to take a nap before classes at 7:00. I was hustling very hard to make it work. I had to.

For many years, I had a job in a retail store and worked my way up to manager. It was a lot of work. The store would be very busy, and I would take my sali to the back and pray. At the time, I lived in a place with few Muslims. I had to drive far for a masjid. It was more difficult to practice then, but that made me appreciate my diin more and hold on to it tighter. One day I had a conversation with someone, and they asked if I would be interested in being an interpreter. I considered it and became a medical interpreter. I fell in love with interpreting because I'm constantly with sick people and it humbles me. You learn to be a grateful person because you see everyday people dealing with illness and mortality, and you're reminded of the fragility of life. Some don't have families and rely on interpreters for comfort, and you bond with them. It's when people are most vulnerable. They might ask something, and I can comfort them with the words of Allah (سبحانه وتعالى). It is all I can do. Just be gentle, listen, and offer a kind word and hope. "I know you're sick. I know it's very difficult to keep praying. Hold on to your diin. When you're most vulnerable, keep doing what you're doing." It brings me joy to be able to be with them and encourage them. If this wasn't my life, I would take everything for granted and be disconnected from reality, from how fleeting life truly is.

People always ask me, "Did you have a plan? You have to plan." And I say, "No, I don't plan anything." What I do is consistency. When you plan, it's planning to be prepared to fail. Like, because I planned, I'm giving myself an excuse if I fail. Things didn't go according to plan: oh well, I give up. Because when I fail, I already planned it. So I might say, "Oh, I'm planning on getting up tomorrow." Rather than saying, "Yeah, Allah (سبحانه وتعالى) give me strength, and I'm gonna get up." So I don't plan. I'm gonna get up, and I'll ask for Allah's permission. It's easy to overwhelm yourself with elaborate plans. Everything is already written. Only Allah (سبحانه وتعالى) can change it. If He's written a certain thing for me and He wants to bless me with something more, then only Allah (سبحانه وتعالى) can change that. I can't do that. But He gives me the ability to worship Him. He gave me that ability to get closer to Him. Because that's a choice. Believe or not believe. I come back to this thought: "What do I need to change for me to keep going so that I don't sink?" This world is an ocean. If I stay above the water, I'm good. And to stay above the water is to hold on to Allah (سبحانه وتعالى).

I was saved from suffering and despair the moment I realized my life is not my life but, rather, it's according to how Allah (سبحانه وتعالى) designated my life. That's when I knew that it's not about me. But Allah (سبحانه وتعالى) comes first. It's not just what I want. It's what Allah (سبحانه وتعالى) allows or facilitates for me in His world.

It's important to give back to others. But it doesn't have to be solely money or an elaborate gesture. For me, giving back to my community can happen wherever I am, and I break it down. Every hour, every moment I have, if I can share one good thing, I will share it. Whatever that good thing is, Allah (سبحانه وتعالى)

knows. It's also about how you carry yourself and act by example. Perhaps somebody sees it and is inspired or reminded to do
good. Being a role model is important. You can serve the community by being an example. If someone says, "I can't do that,"
show them they're wrong by being the example that they can.

My dream is to be able to touch one person during a difficult
moment. Whether they read my story and are moved or have
met me in person, I want to be able to touch someone's heart.
For example, if a person is struggling with hijab and I gave them
a different perspective. I know it's not glamorous, and it may not
be easy to wear, but it changed my life for the better when I began wearing it. Or if I motivate someone to acknowledge and
appreciate their parents' journeys and sacrifices. I also dream of
going to Hajj. I have never gone before, and I would love to. It's
something I've prayed that I'm able to do in this lifetime.

Something I've noticed in America is the high level of con-
sumerism. I worked at a place where all we did was figure out
how to get into people's pockets. It went into the way we deco-
rate this or that, change a wall hanging in order to get someone's
attention or put ideas in their head. You're being advertised to
since birth. Wear this, eat that, drink this, or drive that. In a con-
sumerist culture, one's entire self-esteem is based on owning
possessions and is created by someone else. Someone else is
making money out of what beautiful means, rather than you
just saying, I am beautiful. Because it's just about getting your
money. You can never reach happiness or fulfillment because
there will always be more things to buy. You become ungrateful
because you constantly have to reinvent yourself. But you can't
invent yourself; you are not an invention—you are a creation.
You are a human being. You are not a commodity. You're not a
vehicle with a new model out every year. You have to say enough
is enough. And that only happens if you're confident with who
you are. You have to know yourself. You don't know that when
you're young. You have to say to yourself, I'm not a product. I am
who I am, Alhamdulilah. I'm okay. I'm healthy. I am who I am.
And nobody can change me. Nobody can alter me. There is no
dress, makeup, car, or product that can change me. If somebody
insults you, you take that insult as insult, but you don't internal-

ize it. You don't carry what someone else thinks of you. That's not who you are. "Yes, my teeth are crooked: so what?" You can hurt me only if I allow you to; I don't have to give you permission to disrespect me.

~

There are differences in how we raise kids in this country compared to how we approach childrearing in Somalia. For example, kids are expected to be kids, not meddle in or be troubled with adults' problems. Our parents did not come to us with their problems; they shielded that from us. It simply wasn't our business. Our job was to go to dugsi, play, and just be kids. I'm grateful our parents were intentional about not making us grow up too fast.

I'm sympathetic to this young generation of parents who are educated, work, make money, but are unhappy. They're miserable. The homelife doesn't add up because they are overwhelmed and frantic. "The kids are crying; the house is not clean; I have work in the morning. It's so overwhelming, and I need help." When you need help, you cannot offer help to others because you are depleted.

Our parents showed affection in their actions. I would feel funny if my mom said, "I love you." I know my mom loved me by the way she talked to me, how she held me, the way she remembered me when I wasn't there. Love was in her cooking, in her touch, how she came around me when I was sick. When I traveled, she would call me all the time and ask, "Where are you at? How about now?" Because she could not wait for me to get home. I felt her love thousands of miles away.

Imagine a scenario where a single mom comes to America with five kids. Only God knows what struggles she faced to make that journey and raise them in this country for the promise of opportunity. She says to herself, *People are not gonna keep me down. I'm gonna take care regardless, because it's not about me. It's about these children.* And then the next generation grows up, gets married, and has kids that they cannot manage to take care of. But they have the audacity to tell their parents, "You don't know what you're talking about." Is it that the older generation doesn't know, or is it that you don't understand? That's an important difference. These parents have a world of experience. Sometimes that experience is more precious and useful than any college degree. My proof is, when you graduate college, they train you for a job. Why can't they just give you the job and say, go do it? Because the experience counts. So these people have so much wisdom from experience to share, but we discount it because they don't speak English. English doesn't make people what they are. Just because they don't speak English doesn't mean they don't comprehend. Value, worth, and credibility are not tied to one language. It would be a very dull world if they were.

Unfortunately, we tear ourselves up. We don't give ourselves credit. We look down on each other. We look down on our parents, like they don't know anything. If they don't know anything, you're nothing. Because you came from them. So what does that make you? Why do you think you are where you are? How did you get here? If they're nothing, how did you get yourself here?

So that their kids could survive and have a better life, this generation had to call home and hear that their parents died. They haven't seen their family since they left home. Ten years, twenty years go by, and they can't get in touch. Somebody calls you and says, "So-and-so died." They say, "Okay. May Allah (سبحانه وتعالى) have mercy on them." But they're still intact; you live. This resiliency is a gift. You have to give Allah (سبحانه وتعالى) that strength. And say, "Allah (سبحانه وتعالى), thank you." And then you say to your parents, "Thank you." Because that strength they instill in you.

You didn't fall apart because they give you that ability to be a rock. Anything can happen to you, but they prepared you for that. As sure as tomorrow comes, one by one, we will die. But this is the legacy I'm leaving behind. Be intact. Be a rock. Whatever comes, whatever you see, don't let yourself fall apart. You're stronger than that. Stay intact. Be unapologetic about who you are. That's where it comes from, that resilience. Wear your hijab. Pray. Don't be apologetic for your own given rights. You don't have to explain. If somebody says, "Why do you . . ." I don't have to explain it to you. You're not entitled to know.

I have four brothers and two sisters. My dad favored the girls and believed his girls could do no wrong. Outside of that, my parents didn't prefer one kid over the others. When it comes to double standards in the home, our parents were very fair. I also think it's about how we view a situation. If we're looking for something, we'll find it. Girls and boys have different roles and responsibilities, but our parents loved us the same, and we knew they wanted the best for us. I do find that parenting in America is a unique challenge. Our value system is being undermined. For example, if your daughter wears hijab, she's constantly having to explain to people why she wears it. Other people might say, "Why do you wear that? Men don't cover. You're oppressed." And now she's in a defensive state and might become insecure about her culture and religion because it's not the norm; it is foreign. If she doesn't have the language or confidence to be different, she might come to resent her parents and culture. It's like slowly being fed a poison.

On the topic of sex, boys and girls are raised differently in our households. My parents were definitely more protective of me because I was a girl. A parent's number-one goal is to prepare their kids for their futures. Our parents show us by example. There are certain responsibilities a man will have, and that's for a man to teach his sons. Likewise, there are certain responsibilities a woman will have, and that's for a woman to teach her daughters. A man can't teach a girl how to be a woman; a woman can't teach a boy how to be a man. When a household doesn't have a father, there's no example for how to be a man. One day that son will grow up. Who can he look up to? Who taught him how to be a husband, treat his wife, and be a father to his children? The mother will instill everything in her daughter. And the daughter will surpass her brother because she has a role model.

The daughter will still experience hardships. She will learn self-reliance and independence from her mom, because that's how she was raised. She wants to control everything; she got her strength from her mom. She knows how to do everything by herself, for herself. So even though she hates being the provider and the nurturer, the wife and the husband, the man and the woman, even though she has that same resilience and hates what her mother did, she will repeat the same thing to her own kids. She doesn't know when to stop; as the daughter of a single mother, she's in competition with her husband.

This is an important difference between before, in Somalia, and here, after Somalia. Nearly every household had a mother and a father; there was no misunderstanding about our responsibilities and duties. Fathers were providers and respected for it. Now a child may say, "Why should I care about my dad? Why should I respect him? He doesn't do anything." They don't recognize his contributions to the household and family. You have to respect because that is a life commandment. After Allah (سبحانه وتعالى) gave the command and says, "Do not associate," He says, "Respect parents." And respecting doesn't mean that your parents are wrong and because they are wrong you punish them. No. Then you're wrong, because you lowered your ways and they are your parents. So you're not over-suppressing them, the wrong they did, because they are human beings. Give them a chance. They might come back and apologize for their wrong. If they don't, you forgive them anyway. Because there's a lack of knowledge. They cannot offer what they don't have. You can't resent somebody for not knowing something they don't know.

When you have that cohesion, there's a balance in the home. Parents can be intentional about how they're raising their kids. There is a danger of having more kids than you can raise. The problem is that now the children must raise the children. "I'm gonna have all this many babies, and you're gonna help me to take care of them." When you get married, pray that Allah (سبحانه وتعالى) grants you the ability to withhold and take care of your household, because this is something you will be asked about on Yawm al-Qiyamah. What did you do with your kids when they were young? How did you train them to become who they are? Because they are my responsibility. So if I'm too overwhelmed, I am gonna force my daughter to raise my kids. That's not fair to her, your kids, or you. As a mother, I should know what is bothering my kids. I should pay attention to their needs and be present in their lives. Sometimes we say, anyone can have a child, but not everyone can be a parent. Parenting is a gift.

You're not born with it, but it's something you practice and work on intentionally. You think about these things before you have kids. If I've been single my whole life and I'm a messy person, if I get married and have kids, will that transform me into an organized person? No, you have to know what you're bringing in. "A house is not built without a foundation." Work today on being the type of person you want to be tomorrow.

It's also important not to resent your parents. For example, a daughter might resent her single mom. It's not fair to your mom, because your mom chose to stay and it's your father who left. He walked out on his responsibility, and the whole family will pay the price for it. We let him get away with it and blame her. But the mom, as flawed as she is, is doing her best given the circumstances. We lower the standard for the father because he is not present, and we raise the standard for the mom to something she will never be able to reach, because she cannot be both parents. So maybe someone thinks, "My dad, who rarely sees me, offers to take me out to dinner, and it's the best thing that ever happened. My mom is here for me and brings me a snack; I will disparage it." But she tried her best, and that is more than we can say for a father who abandons his children.

Another issue families are up against is that kids are being taught to mistrust and belittle their parents. When we were growing up, we were raised to respect our parents and trust that they loved us and had our best interests at heart. We had our roles: they were the parents and we were the kids. But in American culture and at this time, it's a different experience altogether. At school, teachers teach kids to question and critique their cultures, faith, and family, but not to question teachers and their institution. They are taught that parents, siblings, and family can't understand the real you, but your friends completely understand you. This makes no sense. When you go to jail, when you get sick, or when someone dies, who is there for you? Your mom and family. Friends are the first to leave when the going gets tough, but you want to cut off the only person who will never leave you and has been there since before you remember?

Your family is your foundation; when you can't trust or understand them, who do you turn to? You need to be separated in order to be divided. We're taught to question the parents' motives. "Your mother didn't wear hijab growing up; why should you?" "Why do you listen to Qur'an? Your mom doesn't even know how to read the Qur'an, but she takes you to dugsi." Instead of being grateful for being given what she did not have or learning what she did not learn, you're taught to be suspicious. Kids are constantly told to follow your heart, to do your own thing, that parents don't understand you, that old people don't understand you—how could they ever relate to you? Kids are bombarded with media and schools telling them to belittle their culture, their faith, and who they are. Then they start to look at their parents like they are backward. Uncivilized. They're uneducated. They don't know anything. I know better than them. And then that disconnects you from them. Then in turn, they cannot give you that knowledge and the values that parents should pass from their elders. This idea is so antithetical to our culture because wisdom is passed down from elders to the young. So if the young can't trust and learn from the elders, where does that wisdom go? You look at your parents like they are no good.

You cannot learn from people you look down on. So instead of learning from and listening to your parents, you're convinced you need to go to someone you can respect, someone with college degrees. They tell you your parents are all wrong; they shouldn't say this, and they shouldn't say that. You become mesmerized; you nearly melt. Finally, someone who gets it! But this whole time, you've overlooked, condescended to, and disrespected the right people who were there all along. The ones who love you. The ones who want you to be unstoppable; the ones who would even give you their hearts and die for you. How can you get information from somebody who doesn't know you? They don't know anything about you. Your mom raised you. She carried you. She knows what you're good at and what you're not. She even knows when you're lying to her! And it starts when you tell your parents, "You don't know this. You don't know that. You don't know . . ."—and what that really means is, "I don't want to hear you. And I don't want anything to do with you. You're not as smart as me."

When you turn on a TV and the news is full of stereotypes or when you feel discriminated against at school or in the workplace and people are saying all this stuff about you that isn't true, who is going to reaffirm you? "This is our faith." Or, "You have a question? Let me answer it for you." Will they, those so-called experts, do that for you? No. They think our history started in 1991. "Let me tell you all about us. Let me tell you about our tradition. Let me tell you the beauty of our culture." You can't even talk to that person because you already decided this person is less than you are.

Despite that, your parents still know you. First of all, what connects you with your parents is Islam. Any Muslim, anywhere, you're connected to because of that. The parent is connected to their child because Allah (سبحانه وتعالى) gives that ability. Your mom carried you for nine months. She barely slept when you were born. After she put you down, she knew you were hungry before you even started crying. That's how close she is to you. It's a mercy from Allah (سبحانه وتعالى). The second thing is that Mom is always there, no matter how hard life gets, through thick and thin. No one else is. You do not get old for your mom. You don't age for your mom. You're always the same person from the moment she breastfed you up until now; you're that person. You do not get smart and grow up in her eyes. When she's looking at you, you're always that baby. You can have a PhD, but you are her baby.

Like I always tell every child, you obey the Owner of the world, and He brings you the world. You chase the world alone, and you will be left behind. And you will never get other than what He has written for you.

I would suggest to parents that they teach their child the love of Allah (سبحانه وتعالى). Don't teach the child to associate Islam with punishment. What you're doing is teaching them to hate the diin and to run from it. You teach the love to attract the love. Remember that compulsion in diin. Allah (سبحانه وتعالى) has granted us free will, so grant your children that. Teach your children how to love Allah (سبحانه وتعالى) the way they love you.

Because then His love is higher than everything. When they know Allah (سبحانه وتعالى), they love Allah (سبحانه وتعالى), and they will find happiness. Don't teach your child to practice Islam for the sake of others but instead for their own hearts.

If I love you and I enjoy you and I want to be around you, it doesn't matter the specifics of what you say. I want to be around you, right? I call you. I think whatever you say is a jewel because I love you. The same goes for understanding the message of the Qur'an. When I know Allah (سبحانه وتعالى) and I love him, then I will contemplate His words. I will understand the beauty of the Qur'an. I will understand what Allah (سبحانه وتعالى) is asking me for. What is He asking; what does He want from me? Not what my mom wants. Because the Qur'an is talking to everyone; we just have to listen. When you pick up your kids from dugsi, ask them, "What did you learn today? What was the benefit?" If a child says, "I can't memorize," say, "Don't memorize. It's okay. Keep listening. Allah (سبحانه وتعالى) will make it easy for you. But what did you learn today? How did you implement what you learned?" Engage them. You can memorize the whole Qur'an, but if the words don't go past your lips, what did you gain?

Give your kids choices. You have to sit with the child, say, "How was the dugsi? How do you feel? What do you think about dugsi? Do you like dugsi?" Ask them if they have enough time to be a kid and play. You might say, "I don't want to take all your Saturdays and Sundays. Or do you want to do the dugsi this way?" Work with them and find what works for them. You want them to feel comfortable and to love what they're doing, not resent it. Talk to your kids. We need to stop doing what society expects us to do. I am not other people. I'm not this person's house. I'm not this person's backyard. I have my own life, and my children should have their own life. Stop competing and comparing.

Lead by example. Say I'm busy and somebody is calling. The child answers and says to me, "It's so-and-so. They want to talk to you." If I tell my child, "Tell her I'm not here," I'm teaching a lie. But if my child dodges my calls tomorrow and tells a friend, "Pick up the call and tell her I'm not here," I'm the one to blame.

We're the ones who taught them. If I'm honest with my child, my child is gonna be honest with me.

At least once a day, sit and talk with your kids. Have conversations with them. When you're cooking, teach the child and say, "You know, when I was young, this is how I used to do with my mom. This is what we used to eat. This is how my mom used to discipline." Teach your child how your mom was disciplining you. Teach your child how kind your mom was. Teach, because then you're telling them where you come from. Tell them about grandma, their dad, how you were raised, and teach that history. Let them ask questions and go back and forth. You are creating a line of communication.

We cannot deal with our children as we did in Somalia. I grew up in Somalia. If I would have had a child and they were born in America, then they grew up in America. So I need to understand my child's thinking and culture. Their identity may be Somali, but their mind is American. I need to learn how to communicate with my child. The teachers have eight hours with him. He's being programmed. So I need to un-program him in order for him to understand me. It's the same thing with showing love. Kids in this country need to hear "I love you." It was odd to us back home but is necessary here. So we adapt. You don't have to say it in English; say it in Somali. But make sure the kid understands that you're showing love.

～

I was abroad when the Civil War started. The president spoke out and announced the war, but it didn't feel real; I couldn't digest it. By then, I was living in the States and most of my siblings were in Europe. My parents and relatives were still in Mogadishu, and they fled to Nairobi. The war was so different from my idyllic memories of my hometown. People were fleeing; so many were displaced. *Okay, it's a civil war*, I thought to myself. *Yeah, but maybe it will get better.* My dad passed away not long after.

We still have the same problems to this day. Everyone wants to present their own tribe. Everybody cannot be a president. We have to come together and pick just one. What I've noticed about our community is that we are very protective against outsiders. But inside, we destroy ourselves. Because we express ourselves orally, we like to talk. But there's a saying that a little knowledge is very dangerous. We know a little bit about something, and then we make all these assumptions and we don't know what we're talking about. Everybody has to have their say. Even to this day, that's the problem.

~

Growing up, I was raised Somali. I only identified as Black later, because it wasn't how I was raised to view myself. If you're looking at me, you see that I'm Black. So I don't need to point out, "I'm Black." Ethnicity is where you come from, it's your DNA. Somalis can have a lighter, medium, or dark color; there is no one shade. When I'm being asked, "Who are you?" straight out from my heart the answer is Somali. It doesn't have American in it. It doesn't have anybody else. It's just Somali. It's strange to fill out a demographic questionnaire and everybody has a hyphen, a qualifier, except for White people. Are they not White Americans? Even the natives have Native American, and this land is theirs.

I have to stress that culture is not just the outside. It's not just food, language, clothes, furniture, or architecture. It's about our values. That's what matters. It's easy to shed that outside layer of culture. I can wear jeans and a turban. But what about the way I view the world, my people, and myself? What about the questions I ask? The assumptions I make? The things I value? My manners, beliefs, and faith?

When you come to America, don't think you have to change your whole identity and compromise who you are. You don't have to erase your identity. Have courage to remain true to who you are.

~

To anyone who is struggling: No matter what it is, do not ever forget the mercy of Allah (سبحانه وتعالى). No matter what you've done, stop judging your past self and look ahead to the future. Do not speak for Allah (سبحانه وتعالى) and His plan of attack; just turn to Him. Look at the generosity of Allah (سبحانه وتعالى). Do not constrict the mercy of Allah (سبحانه وتعالى).

To Somali people: One thing I will tell my community is that they underestimate who they are. They are so generous, so beautiful, so giving. So, stop looking at people's faults and promote people's goodness. Because they have a lot to give. When you have a lot to give, do not focus on what you can't do. Focus on what you can give. Because you have so much to offer. Just concentrate on the goodness of the people and what we can do together. And what we can do together is unstoppable.

To Somali women: I tip my hat to you. You are beautiful. Mothers are resilient, brilliant, talented, beautiful inside and out, no matter what community they're in, no matter where they are. So, keep doing it, and don't let anyone degrade you or tell you anything other than that. Push your kids. Be there for your kids. Know your kids. Learn your kids. And build your kids' self-esteem. Keep telling your kids all the time what they're good at, instead of saying what they're not good at. Build them up.

To Somali men: Remember, every Somali woman has a Somali man as a father. So, when Somali women do good, it's because they had a Somali father. You are a part of that success because you are the fathers of those women. You are also part of the Somali society. So therefore, do not always think you're not good enough. You are good enough because Allah (سبحانه وتعالى) gave you that title. You are good because you are the fathers of those good mothers and good fathers. The Somali home is the home of a father and mother. Let's be there for our children. Not only one person, but both. Whether you are with their mother or not, you are the father of those children. So make sure you stand with your children and you support them, no matter what.

12

Shukriya Abdirahman, 80s, Jigjiga, Ethiopia
pseudonym

I was born in Jigjiga, a city in the Ogaden region, which was once a part of Somalia. Colonialists intervened and gave away to the Ethiopians land that was not theirs to give. Somalis tried to regain independence in the war of '77 but were not successful. We've been torturously oppressed by their regime. Men were killed, women raped, and unspeakable atrocities were done to our people.

I was raised by my mother; I never met my father. I grew up with eight siblings, all of whom have now passed. We lived on the outskirts of the city, in baadiya. Because of that, we didn't attend formal school or dugsi. We learned what we could from our families. Eventually, the violence was so unbearable that we left our home. We had only our mother, and she alone could not protect us from the brutal soldiers. We were in constant danger. We had no choice but to flee to Mogadishu. My mother wanted us to have safety and education, both unattainable in our current condition.

We lived in Xamar for many years, until the war of '91. I had livestock then, and a home. We made a living for ourselves, but then we had to flee. I lost all my livestock. The irony was that we had fled to Mogadishu for safety, and we now had to leave Mogadishu for safety. We were refugees once again. I had to drag my sister's corpse. I had my sandals in my hand running away. Someone stopped me and asked for my sandals, and I gave them away. I didn't own a single thing. I met another family fleeing, and I was able to get sandals from them. They also gave me a bit of meat.

I thought about Siad Barre, who let our country descend into madness. We were told to accept him because he was Darood. But he was not a good leader. What kind of leader would allow that to happen? The present is no better for us. People back home live in fear of violence. We've been oppressed from both sides. To the west, the Ethiopians, and to the east, Al-Shabaab. If it wasn't for them, we would be able to live peacefully in our beautiful country. There is an abundance of wealth in the land and a chance for prosperity. That's why everybody wants our land.

We lived in Kenya for some time before I came to America. I first came to Minnesota and was placed in Faribault. The paperwork was not completely sorted, so I was sent to San Diego instead. I decided to go back to Jigjiga. I lived there for some time before I became very sick with bronchitis. The health care back home is not great, so I came back to the United States. It cost a lot of money to come here, over $2,000 for the plane ticket alone. I came here because I had health complications and needed health care.

To this day, I still do not have health insurance. I don't understand why I was denied. I have filled out so much paperwork and have worked with many interpreters, but no one has helped me. I keep filling out form after form, but nothing happens. Instead, I keep being told my card is closed. The last time I heard from the insurance, I was told I need to go to a building in St. Paul to fix my case, but who will take me? How will I get there? I live by myself in this small apartment, and I can't drive or take the bus. I've had problems with my back since I was forty-one and have trouble moving and getting around.

A lady and her daughter worked with me for months and took me down to the welfare office to help me get assistance. I was denied then too. I'm exhausted from trying. Eventually I was able to get $200 a month for food; that's the only welfare I've ever received. Now they've cut it down to $170, and I don't know why they did that. Alhamdulilah, I'm still here.

I have no one to look after me and take care of me. Most days,

I am by myself in this cramped apartment. The only one who helps me is Allah (سبحانه وتعالى). My daughters live in the suburbs, far away from the city. They have full-time jobs and many children and cannot look after me every day. For a long time, I did not know how to use my cell phone, so I could not call them. I can't read or write, so I can't call them by dialing their numbers or using caller ID. I can only pick up their phone calls. Someone recently programmed speed dial on my phone and now I can call them with the press of a button.

I have many health problems. I need to monitor my blood pressure every day, but I do not know how to count so I don't understand what the numbers on the machine mean. I had a niece come by and read it for me, but she's become busy with school or work and doesn't come around anymore. Sometimes people come by and bring me muufo or onions or tomatoes. It's nice when they visit.

I don't have my citizenship yet. I have already filed the paperwork. They said I have to wait five months, and it's been two months so far. Once I get my citizenship, I will immediately apply for a passport. I cannot wait to leave this country. It is miserable here. It's not a good place to be. If this place didn't have such cold, brutal winters, it might have been tolerable.

I detest the food in this country. I don't cook here or eat anything from the fridge. The food has no flavor. It does not taste like food. Milk that is not our milk. Meat that is not our meat. Food that is not our food. The food we used to cook back home— you would not believe the goodness. Our food had such richness in the aromas, flavors, and textures of those divine meals. It is not something you could ever compare to here. You would think the milk here is produced from trees. It may as well be. There's no way a cow could produce this milk.

There's no life for me in this country. It's very lonely in this apartment. My eighty-seven-year-old friend recently died alone. Young people here have all the opportunities right in front of them. You can learn their language and adapt to any situation. Work hard and pursue an education. You can better yourselves and create a life for yourselves to take you anywhere. You can survive here. What can I do as an elderly woman? I can't speak their language, read or write, or move around the city. I am entirely at the mercy of others.

Sometimes young men come to the building and help around with elderly men. But no one comes to help us elderly women. Young people could help if they wanted. It doesn't take much: food, company, going to a doctor's appointment. But we could surely use the help. Instead, it feels like we've been forgotten or cast aside. Maybe we could have found a way back home, but here, we need the help of others. This isn't our country, is not our land. It's different.

My children live all over the world. I have daughters who live nearby, as well as children in Jigjiga and London. My sons don't do anything for me. One of my sons is addicted to khat and doesn't do much. My daughters help when they can. One of my daughters has seven kids and a disabled husband. She tries her best but has a lot on her plate. All of my daughters are married with many children. One of my granddaughters was an interpreter and used to come by but settled down and hasn't visited in a while. When I ask my daughters or grandchildren to come by, they say they have to tend to their kids. I wish someone would help me fix my health insurance or take me to the grocery store. It's a struggle, but I persevere. What else can I do?

I tell my children that this place is no place to have a family. The trouble never stops. There is always something going on or something stacking up. Young people are in the best position out of all of us. My advice to young people would be to go to school and work very hard on your education. Then find a job and work very hard at making money and becoming very skilled. Then when you have something saved up, go back home. The children here are forsaken. Your faith is at risk. It is an extremely hard life. It is bad for your soul. For those who choose to stay, your kids will not listen to you and will be totally lost. Their minds have already been corrupted by this culture and lifestyle. They don't know the difference between up or down; why do you think they will listen to you when you try to guide them? It is a waste of your effort. Take my advice.

The number-one reason people will come here and stay is because they believe they can make money here. That is not true. This is a different kind of poverty from the one we know, but it is still a poverty nonetheless. Even if you make money, it is not a guarantee that it will have barakah and you will gain from it. Is money worth the souls of your children? This is not a country to raise kids in, because there are always problems. I advise people to make their money and leave. But even still, remember that money is not happiness. You will see someone who has never had a penny and has never been in this country who is happy and content. That person has their faith, dignity, and purpose. Rizq is always with Allah (سبحانه وتعالى). When I get back home, my service to the people will be telling people to not go to America. It's not at all what they said it would be.

The youth are losing their culture. They don't carry themselves the same way at all. They look Somali, but they don't have a Somali mind. They've allowed American culture to rob them of their own unique traditions. Their parents need to do a better job explaining things to them, because you can't take for granted that they understand our ways. "This is why we do this, this is how you wear this, this is how we do this," and so on. But we can only do so much. It's up to God, not up to us. Parents can teach and guide, but will their kids listen to them? Will they take that advice? Usually not. You cannot make someone listen to you.

When you come to a new country, there is so much for you to learn. It's one thing for people to adapt to a new place. Everyone should adapt. It is another thing entirely to adapt to a new place and leave behind your own culture and faith. You must have some pride and dignity about where you came from and who you are.

~

I advise that young women do not get caught up in the little details when it comes to finding a husband. Race does not matter, but religion does. Look for a good man who is strong in his diin. Make sure you strengthen your own faith and become knowledgeable. Don't reject a man because he doesn't have a lot. A rich man may someday lose his wealth, and a poor man may someday gain wealth. Money is not an object as long as he can provide. Be very careful about the decision you make; take your time with it. Finally, when you have kids in this country, be prepared to leave. Take your kids and go. In this country, you cannot do it all. Your attention will fall on either your kids or your money, but you cannot do both. Your husband can stay and send money to you. You have to do what's best for the kids. Three or four kids is enough.

I can't give advice to boys. They don't listen to their mom, and they don't even listen to their father.

Somali people, stick to your religion and culture. Don't lose your way. Don't forget who you are. Ask God for forgiveness. Stick together.

13

Sahro Ali, 60s, Baraawe, Somalia
pseudonym

I was born and raised on the coast of Somalia, in a town called Baraawe. I came from a big family with thirteen siblings. Our parents owned a store to make a living. My siblings and I went to school every day. It was very important to our family. After school, my brothers ran along to play soccer with the other neighborhood boys. Meanwhile, my sisters and I swam in the ocean. We all knew how to swim at a very early age. You had to know, because if you didn't, you would be left out. We did a lot of chores around the house, but we also played a lot.

We had a lot of responsibilities growing up. My mother imparted her knowledge and wisdom on me. She was always teaching me one thing or another. Before I knew how to cook, I was sent out to the market to buy ingredients. I would come back and watch her prepare a meal from scratch. I paid attention to what spices she used, if she cooked a vegetable in her own way, and any other little tips and tricks. I still remember the way my mother cooked special dishes for special occasions and visiting guests. My mother was a wonderful cook. She also taught me how to care for a home and how to raise children.

I attended primary and middle school. I was a diligent student. I enjoyed going to school, and even though my teachers were tough, I liked to work hard and earn good marks. I was always competing with my brothers and sisters over who would get the highest grades. We were also very competitive with each other about anything we could come up with. I eventually left school when I got married. My husband and I were paired in an arranged marriage. I didn't know a thing about courtship or marriage at that time. Our families got together and worked it out. He had gone to his father and asked to marry me, and the rest was sorted.

After I became married, we set off for a nearby town. We eventually came back to our hometown. My husband opened a small business. I took care of the household and raised our children. We had ten kids, all born in Somalia. We lived in Baraawe for a while before we were sponsored and immigrated to the United States. We left Somalia before the war began. We heard many sad stories over the phone. Of course, our families were still there, and we were very worried. Most of them were able to flee.

A few years ago, I was able to visit my country for the first time since I had left, over twenty years before. I felt a mix of emotions. I was very grateful to be back home. I saw some people I hadn't seen in many years. I couldn't believe how old they looked. Of course it had been a long time, but their appearance was also due to the sun beating down on them and a lifetime of struggle. My younger siblings looked older than I did.

But it wasn't only the people that looked different. I could not recognize the place I had come from. The city looked different from the plane, but to experience it in person was another thing entirely. I could not recognize the home I was born in, or the one I raised my children in. The neighborhoods looked very different. I felt like I had landed in a different place. There were so many new buildings and houses. I could not stay long because I had to tend to things back in America. I returned two more times since my first visit. I'm a little bit more used to it now, but it's still confusing and shocking to see in person.

We came to the United States in 1990 and were placed in Virginia. There was a growing Somali community at that time. My husband worked as a cab driver, and I stayed at home with the kids. I worked odd jobs here and there along the way. I mostly sold goods to other women in the neighborhood and community. After a while, we decided to move to Minnesota. We made the choice because we wanted better opportunities for the children and for them to attend excellent dugsi programs. Minnesota also had good health care and assistance programs. We wanted to be in a large Somali community. Minnesota does have very cold winters, but every place has its own good and bad. Overall, it was a better opportunity.

Culture and religion are very important to us. It's our obligation to pass that down to the next generations. I have ten children and eight grandchildren. My kids can all speak Somali well, but my grandkids struggle with it. They can understand me, but their instinct is to speak English to each other and their parents. Pretty soon they will lose the language altogether. They speak English all day at school, watch American television, and speak it to each other. When do they speak Somali? It has to start at home.

Language is like a muscle: you have to use it or it will wither away. When my grandchildren speak English to me, I tell them, "Maya, af Soomaali ku hadal." When they are at my house, they can only speak Somali. I often tell my children to stop letting their children speak English at home. As parents, they should enforce that rule. Once children forget, you can't teach them again, so it's best if they don't lose their mother tongue now, when they're young.

~

Education is very important. Advancing in your education can allow you to find better opportunities and take care of your family. My advice to girls is to stay in school and take your education seriously. If you work hard in school, you can get very far in life. Take advantage of the opportunities that you have in front of you. Boys and marriage can wait until you're older. When you want to get married, be picky and choose a good, religious man. Don't pick the first guy you meet either. Look around a bit, and take your time making the right choice. The same way you take school seriously, take your diin seriously. Become knowledgeable about Islam; it will only benefit your life. Don't abandon your hijab: it's your protection and obligation. Make dua that Allah (سبحانه وتعالى) makes it easier for you, if you're struggling with it, and pray your salat. That will give you strength. Listen to your parents and show them respect. You will never understand what your parents did for you to be here.

I offer the same advice to young men. The difference with young men is that they are so eager to have a job that they compromise their education. They would rather work and make money right away than struggle for a while in school but gain the opportunity to make more money down the line. That's why there are more girls going to college than boys. But young men need to understand that an education is a sacrifice that pays off. A lot of money later is better than a little money now. You will struggle for a while, but then again, everyone has struggled. It is an unavoidable part of life.

Young people today have lost their culture. They can't speak Somali, they've lost good manners, they dress poorly, and they don't have respect. It's not entirely their own fault. The older ones have been bad role models to them. Ever since they came to this country, they have been acting out. They are loud, fight, and dress up to go to this party or that wedding. What kind of example is that? They've abandoned their traditional clothes and culture for American culture. They should have preserved what they had instead of chasing something they are not.

～

My advice to Somali men is that you should intensely pursue work. Even if it is not easy, keep struggling, and one day it will pay off. The best thing you can do is to pursue a better life for you and your family. To be a man is to be a provider, and you will gain respect if you do that. Take school seriously, better yourself, and be ambitious about your future. You are more than capable.

My advice to Somali people is to stop the fighting and killing. Fear God, first and foremost. We are one people with one culture, one religion, and one language. There is no need to constantly fight or be violent with one another. We cannot move forward and progress if we continue to hurt each other.

Most of my kids are grown up and married now. We still have some kids at home. I spend most of my time at the masjid in dugsi or practicing my ashar. Like every Somali, I've attended dugsi since I was very young. I finished the Qur'an then. I took a break from dugsi when I was raising my kids. Since they are older now, I've had more time to myself. Since then, I've finished the Qur'an twice. I am very dedicated to learning more and taking advantage of my time. It's a great blessing in my life that I am able to spend time studying the Qur'an.

14

Ubax Yussuf, 90s, Bosaso, Somalia
pseudonym

I was born and raised in Bosaso. I had ten siblings, two of whom are living in the United States. The rest of my siblings are in various places across the Horn and Europe.

My father owned a store; he was one of the wealthier men of our neighborhood. Both of my parents died when I was a teenager. While I was growing up, we moved between cities and baadiya. We owned livestock and tended to the land.

When we lived in the city, my siblings and I attended school. We studied very hard and took our education very seriously. Back then, if you were very proficient, you could become a teacher after a certain grade. Two of my brothers were at the top of their class, so they became teachers. If you didn't do well, the teachers would hit you.

It's very different to how it is now in this country. I've noticed that kids don't take education as seriously. It's a different business entirely. I'm not sure why kids are not as interested in their studies. We knew that the only way to make something of your life was by going to school and being excellent. They also are not taught as rigorously as we once were. My great-grandchildren are learning math that we would've mastered before their age. I thought the education in this country would be better, but it is not.

I got married when I was seventeen. I was paired with a young man with a good family and money. That was the way back home. Your tribes and fathers talked with one another and came to an arrangement. They had to determine if it was a good fit, and the elders are wise so they will make a good choice. I had five kids and many more grandchildren and great-grandchildren.

I moved to Xamar soon after I was married, and we lived there for many years. Xamar was a beautiful city with good people. The hustle and bustle of the city combined with the beauty of the ocean. My husband owned a business, and I tended to the household and raised the kids. I had family in the city, so I was never alone; we always had visitors. My cousins or aunts would visit me and keep me company.

Then the war came on suddenly. We weren't expecting it. Our lives were turned upside down overnight. The nights were the hardest. The gunshots got closer and closer to us. We made a decision to leave before the chaos took our lives. We fled to Kenya along with most everyone in our neighborhood who survived. It was hard to start over, but we had our lives and health. We lived in a refugee camp for many years. We knew we had to leave in order to find a better opportunity for our family. We didn't want to be trapped at the camp for the rest of our lives.

We left Kenya for America when George Bush was elected. Looking back, we are lucky we were granted asylum before 2001. It was much harder to immigrate afterward. It was also much harder to sponsor your family. Many people were left behind. Most people claim nationality by birth, but if asked I say I am both Somali and American. And why wouldn't I be American? I have lived here for twenty years. So time has made this my land.

I've had my passport for over ten years. It means a great deal to me because it allows me convenience of travel. I can go back and forth between my countries. I see them both as my homes, one I was born to and one I made a home. I love both countries. I've come to love America because there's no trouble here, in the sense of a war or constant violence. We have good hospitals and get paid well, and those who came before us welcomed newcomers to this country when we first arrived. We had our religion back home, and we still have it here. I am proud of the way we transitioned. We've received great blessings.

I cannot answer where I would rather be or where I will remain. I can only say I will be happy wherever Allah (سبحانه وتعالى) has written for me to be. There is very little we control. Allah (سبحانه وتعالى) determines where we are born, our family, wealth, health, education, and so on. We can only concern ourselves over things we have power over. Otherwise you will go mad attempting to control what is not yours to control. I'm not attached to a street address, apartment number, or neighborhood. I am happy wherever I go. That is the way of our culture; we are easygoing and not easily tied down. The last time I returned to the States, I was uncertain if I should. But I became excited to see my community again.

I would like to tell Somali diaspora that they should embrace their second home. Both Somalia and America can be your country and your home. Remember that when you came to this country you were welcomed by those who came before you. It is then your duty to welcome those who come after you. Don't take that for granted. If you choose to go back home and Allah (سبحانه وتعالى) grants it, then that is your right. If you choose to stay in your new home and Allah (سبحانه وتعالى) grants it, then that is also your right. No matter what you choose, you have to help each other and guide each other toward the right way. Stay firm in your diin and keep our dhaqan alive.

I would advise Somali men and Somali women to never forget the way that you were created by the Creator. Remember back to the way your father treated your mother and the way your mother treated your father. They are good role models for marriage, especially during this time of dysfunction and confusion. Fulfill the rights and obligations you have over one another and grant each other full respect. Men, don't run out on a good woman and mistreat her. Women, take care of your homes and treat a good man right.

Young ladies, you have accomplished a great deal in your education and careers. You live in a country with a lot of distractions and fitnah. You did not learn everything as we did. Even still, attach yourself to your faith and act accordingly. Fear God and embrace your religion. Be good people and examples in your country by conducting yourself in an honorable and respectable way.

I can't say that I ever felt hardship in my religion. I pray my salat, go to the masjid, and live a simple life. Allah (سبحانه وتعالى) made it easy. I held on to my faith from the moment I was brought into this world. Allah (سبحانه وتعالى) has not shown me suffering. When you hold on tight to the diin and ask Allah (سبحانه وتعالى) for help, He makes life easier for you. Allah (سبحانه وتعالى) grants barakah; Allah (سبحانه وتعالى) grants health and rizq. Where you live, Allah (سبحانه وتعالى) brought you to it. Where you will die, Allah (سبحانه وتعالى) will take you there. Recite *Hasbunallah wa ni'mal-Wakil.* It means, "Sufficient for us is Allah, and [He is] the best Disposer of affairs" (Qur'an 3:173). Say this dua often and everything will be easy for you. Ask Him for advice and everything will be made lighter.

I have not experienced any struggle in America. Every place I go to, I have only been welcomed and accepted by my community. God has made this country feel like my first country and home. It would make no difference to me if I lived in a Muslim-majority country. In fact, it is much easier in this country. Why? Back home, we had to do so much work in order to simply live. We had to tend to livestock, gather water from a well far away, and much more. In order to take your studies seriously and learn, you had many obstacles to overcome. The hours of the day were consumed by worldly matters, and little time was left to spend with the Qur'an.

In America, the story is a different matter entirely. Food is very easy to come by, there are no cattle and livestock to herd, and money is easy and quick. We have so many conveniences and comforts. Whereas before we were preoccupied with the matter of day-to-day living. You couldn't put off those things for long. Older folks spend our time in the masjids learning Qur'an at our leisure because all our needs are met and we have a great blessing to do so. Life is simple when you make it simple.

I've visited my grandchildren all over the world. They live across countries such as New Zealand, Denmark, England, and Somalia. They've adapted really well to their homes. They don't share the same perspectives and culture that we have, but that is understandable because they weren't brought up the same way we were. I am happy for them to be well adjusted and to be able to take advantage of the opportunities they have. It is, after all, their country now. But I hope they don't forget the culture and country that their parents left behind. It will be their responsibility to pass it on to the next generation, as they have received it from those before.

The parents raising their kids in the diaspora have their own share of difficulties. Just like in any place, there are good people and bad people. The overwhelming majority of these parents are hardworking people who love their families and are taking care of them. They raise their kids with a good understanding of their cultural heritage and to be upstanding citizens. They work very hard at both providing for their children and raising them to be good Muslims who benefit those around them.

The greatest achievement for a person is to be able to do something for themselves and to contribute to their country. How can one attain this? First, work hard at becoming an excellent student. Be the best student you can be, and learn from those wiser than you. Then use those skills to work hard in your profession. When the time comes, use those skills and resources to contribute to your country. You will be able to greatly impact the lives of a great number of people. You will be rewarded for it, not only in this life but in the next. Everyone is capable of contributing in their own way. It's up to you to find out how you can do so. And then eventually, you will be able to share your wisdom and insights with other people. What a good life to lead.

Acknowledgments

The creation of this book was made possible with the support of countless people. I will attempt to acknowledge the efforts of those people in no particular order. A special thank-you to those whom God placed in my path and who aided this project without my knowledge.

None of this would have been possible without Allah (سبحانه وتعالى). No words could encapsulate my gratitude. Allahu Akbar.

Thank you to Kaltun Karani, Qorsho Hassan, Amran Farah, Anisa Ali, and Roun Said. Thank you to all the women who lent their stories, wisdom, and lessons without sharing their names. You believed in the vision of the book and selflessly allowed us to share in deeply personal parts of your lives. Thank you for trusting me to tell your story sincerely. May Allah (سبحانه وتعالى) reward you infinitely.

A special thank-you to my editor, Ann Regan. Your thoughtfulness, dedication, and tireless support made this possible.

Thank you to Mary Benner. Your help in transcribing interviews was vital in bringing this book to life.

Thank you to the Minnesota Historical Society Press. Your commitment to preserving and sharing the stories of Minnesotans is commendable. I am grateful for the support provided through the press's Elmer L. and Eleanor Andersen Publications Fund.

To my champions. You've offered immeasurable support and wisdom over the years, and I am a better person for it. To Ramla Bile, Salma Ibrahim, Nekessa Opoti, Saido Abdirashid, Yusra Abdi, Balkis Hassan, Fardosa Ahmed, and Shaykha Aysha Wazwaz.

Thank you to my parents, Fardowsa Ali and Abdirahman

Adan. In part, I started this book to better understand you. I emerged with an inexpressible admiration, gratitude, empathy, and complete adoration for you both. I will never fully know what you sacrificed to give my siblings and me the best shot at life, but as I grow older, I begin to uncover the wisdom and bottomless love you have given us. Even when we don't see eye to eye, there is never a doubt in my mind that you have my best interest at heart. I say to readers, if you have benefited from this book or from anything I've done, please pray for my parents.

To my brothers, I'm lucky to have you. Thank you for being the sons, husbands, fathers, and brothers we love.

To my beloved sister, Ilhan Dahir. The best gift our parents ever gave me was you. You have fundamentally shaped the woman I am today. It will take a lifetime to emulate your beauty, poise, kindness, charm, nature, humor, temperament, resilience, integrity, and light. Thank you for everything you have done for me. Thank you for everything you are to me.

To my nieces and nephew. Aisha, my heart, may you never lose your light and laughter. Your joy has brought us closer together. Safiya, my little Degan, may you always be as clever and resilient as you are now. Imran, our baby boy, may you be the twinkle in your parents' eyes.

Thank you to my dearest friends. Your support and understanding made this possible. You offered laughter and respite when the going got tough and joy and sincere love in our good times. Thank you Yasmin Abdi, Hanan Karia, and Shukri Abdalla. A special thank-you to my dear friend Muna Abdirahman, who lent her talents to the book's artful cover. I'm so grateful to have each of you in my corner.

Thank you to the educators who challenged me and inspired me to shoot for the moon. Thanks to Ms. Erin Webster, Mr. Brad Tagg, Mr. Abdullahi, Mr. Yassin, Ms. Russell, Mr. Khalid, Ms. Carolyn Holbrook, Ms. Gallus, Ms. Kerns, and Ms. Klaverkamp.

To my aunts, uncles, cousins, and grandparents.

To those who came before us and to those who will come after.

To my community.

Glossary

Acronyms

ACT a standardized test administered by American College Testing, Inc.

ELL English Language Learners.

ESL English as a Second Language.

FAFSA Free Application for Federal Student Aid, a form that college applicants and students complete to determine eligibility for financial aid.

FOB "fresh off the boat"; a new immigrant or refugee.

GED an alternative high school diploma.

GPA grade point average.

HBCU Historically Black College and University.

ICE US Immigration and Customs Enforcement.

MRE meals ready to eat.

PSEO post-secondary enrollment option.

PTSD post-traumatic stress disorder.

SRO student resource officer.

STEM the fields of science, technology, engineering, math.

TBI traumatic brain injury.

Words and Phrases

ﷺ—Sallallahu alayhi wa salaam. May God's blessings and peace be with him.

سبحانه وتعالى—Subhanahu wa ta'ala. May He be praised and exalted.

abaya, abayad—a loose, robe-like dress worn by Muslim women.

abtiris—an oral tradition used to preserve lineage.

Af-Maay—a language related to Somali.

af Soomaali—Somali language.

agoon—an orphan (someone who lacks a mother or father or both).

ajnabi—foreigner, also used in Urdu and Somali languages.

Alhamdulilah—"All praise is due to Allah."

Allahu Akbar—God is greatest.

Allahu naxariisto—Somali phrase meaning "May God have mercy on them."

AlMaghrib Institute—an Islamic studies institute founded in Houston, Texas, that provides courses on Islam.

Al-Shabaab—a terrorist group in Somalia.

amanah—roughly, fulfilling a moral obligation or trust.

amarka illahi—roughly, God's will.

ashar—assignment or homework.

awoowe—grandfather.

ayah—verse, typically referring to verses that make up a chapter in the Qur'an.

ayeeyo—grandmother.

baadiya—rural area.

barakah—blessings, good fortune, prosperity.

baranbuur—traditional Somali dance most common at weddings.

calaacal—to complain or whine.

canjeero—flatbread.

dadka Soomaaliyeed—the Somali people.

Darood—a Somali clan.

dhaqan—culture or tradition.

dhaqan celis—to be sent back home for cultural education.

diin—religion or faith.

dua—a prayer of invocation to God, an act of worship.

dugsi—Islamic studies school or secular school.

dunya—the temporal world that precedes the hereafter.

Eid—Eid al-Fitr and Eid al-Adha are two Muslim holidays.

fajr—the first of the five mandatory Islamic prayers performed daily.

fanaan—an artist or singer.

fitnah—various meanings, used to describe difficulties faced during personal trials.

gabay—a form of poetry.

hadith—various collected accountings of the words, deeds, silent approvals, habits, and actions of the Prophet Muhammad ﷺ.

Hajj—pilgrimage, one of the five pillars of Islam; an obligation for Muslims who are financially and physically able to make pilgrimage at least once in their lifetime to the Kaaba in the sacred city of Mecca in Saudi Arabia.

halaqa—a religious gathering or meeting for the study of Islam and the Qur'an.

haraam—forbidden by Islamic law.

Hibaq—Flower from Heaven.

hijab—a garment that conceals a woman's hair, head, and chest, worn by Muslim women observing an Islamic commandment to cover themselves when in the presence of men who are not part of their immediate family.

Hodan Nalayeh—A Somali Canadian reporter and writer.

hooyo—mother.

huruud—traditional Somali facial masks that often use turmeric.

Illahi—God.

"Illahi baa ka weyn."—"God is bigger than this/them."

insh'Allah—God willing.

istikhara—to seek that which is good, a prayer performed by Muslims in order to gain guidance from Allah (سبحانه وتعالى) on a decision.

janazah—funeral.

jilbaab—a form of hijab characterized by a long, cloak-like garment that reaches the knees in length.

khamaar—a form of hijab that popularly refers to a long scarf draped around the head and across the chest.

khat—a plant native to Ethiopia; its leaves are chewed as a stimulant.

khutbah—a sermon commonly delivered before Jummah (Friday) prayer.

kitab—book; commonly used to refer to the Qur'an in casual context.

macalin, *pl.* **macalamiin**—teacher.

maghrib—the evening prayer performed at sunset.

mahmah—Somali proverb.

Majeerteen—a Somali clan.

Malak al-mawt—Angel of Death.

masjid—mosque, a place of worship for Muslims.

"Maya, af Soomaali ku hadal."—"No, speak Somali."

musallah—an open space in a masjid used for prayer.

muufo—a kind of cornbread.

naxaariis—compassion or mercy.

niqab—a form of hijab with a face veil.

Ogaden—Somali tribe and region.

qabil—tribe or clan.

Qorsho—plan.

Qur'an—the well-preserved sacred scripture in Islam, revealed by the Angel Jibril to the Prophet Muhammad ﷺ.

Rahaweyn—a Somali clan.

Ramadan—holy month in Islam.

rizq—sustenance provided by Allah (سبحانه وتعالى).

Saado Cali—a Somali American singer-songwriter and politician born in Somalia in 1950 and assassinated in Mogadishu in 2014; also Saado Ali Warsame.

salaam—shortened version of Asalaamu alakyum, or to greet with salaam.

salat—one of the five pillars of Islam; an obligation upon all Muslims to pray five times a day, at dawn (fajr), midday (dhur), afternoon (asr), sunset (maghrib), and evening (isha).

sali—prayer rug.

seerah—the Prophetic biography; translates to "a path where someone walks." Commonly refers to the life, guidance, and history of the Prophet ﷺ that Muslims try to emulate.

shaykh, *pl.* **shayukh**—a classically trained Islamic scholar.

"Soomaali miya tahay?"—"Are you Somali?"

Soomaalinimo—a notion of shared culture, language, and faith among Somali peoples.

soor—a Somali dish with a base of maize flour and water that can be sweet or savory.

Sufism—a dimension of Islam that focuses on tazkiya and matters of the heart.

Sunan al-Tirmidhī—hadith collected by al-Tirmidhī.

Sunnah—*a.* an act of worship that is rewarded but not mandatory. *b.* the body of traditional social and legal custom and practice of the Islamic community.

Surah Ar-Rahman—a chapter (surah) of the Qur'an.

Surah Fatiha—a chapter (surah) of the Qur'an.

tarawix—a sunnah (recommended) prayer performed during the month of Ramadan.

tazkiya—an Islamic method of self-development that focuses on purification of the heart and soul.

Ummah—community; refers to the Muslim community.

"Wax walba waa calaf"—"Everything is in fate; it was destined to happen."

Xamar—the local name for Mogadishu.

xawaalad—a business that handles sending and receiving payments or remittances.

Yawm al-Qiyamah—the Day of Resurrection.

About the Author

Ayaan Adan is a user experience designer, author, and community organizer based in the Twin Cities. An advocate for privacy, civil liberties, and accessibility, she has given presentations on design and community organizing at the Minneapolis Institute of Art, Twin Cities Startup Week, the Cato Institute, and Georgetown University. She is committed to making a positive impact in the lives of others through storytelling, design thinking, and community organizing.

The text of *Daughters of Arraweelo* has been typeset in Calluna, a typeface designed by Dutch designer Jos Buivenga and released in 2009 through the exljbris font foundry.

Book design by Wendy Holdman.